When No
Majority
Rules

When No Majority Rules

THE ELECTORAL COLLEGE
AND PRESIDENTIAL SUCCESSION

Michael J. Glennon

Congressional Quarterly Inc.
Washington, D.C.

Printed in the United States of America

Cover design: Ed Atkeson/Berg Design, Albany, New York

Library of Congress Cataloging-in-Publication Data

Glennon, Michael J., 1947-
    When no majority rules : the Electoral College and presidential succession / Michael J.
Glennon.
        p.   cm.
    Includes bibliographical references and index.
    ISBN 0-87187-875-5 (pbk.)
    1. Electoral college- -United States. 2. Presidents- -United States- -Election. I. Title.
JK529.G58   1992
324.6' 3' 0973- -dc20   92-40267
                                                                                        CIP

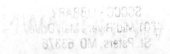

Contents

Preface

In the spring of 1992, when I began writing this book, H. Ross Perot was mounting the most significant third-party challenge for the presidency seen in many years. At times, he was even leading in the polls, ahead of both likely major-party nominees—one of whom was the incumbent president. The popular press, delighted with the newsworthiness of a "volunteer"-supported, folksy-speaking candidate, was rife with "scenarios." Indeed, barely a day went by without some pundit unveiling a new, often outlandish possibility about who might become president *if.* The *if's* varied— *what if* Perot threw his electoral votes to another candidate; *what if* Perot threw the election into the House of Representatives; *what if* the Senate elected a vice president. But the startling realization was always the same: many Americans found that they knew less than they had thought about how the president is chosen *when no majority rules.*

By the fall, when I had finished writing, Perot had withdrawn from and later reentered the presidential race. But by then his popularity had declined, and the *what if* questions had receded into the past. Nevertheless, the roller-coaster events of the summer had clearly revealed the pitfalls of the electoral system. What emerged was the need to understand the system as it existed and to consider reforms in it—preferably in the light of cool, calm reason rather than under the pressure of the next "Perot."

The main object of this book, then, is to explain the process of presidential selection. As vast as the literature is on this subject, it offers little that simply but comprehensively describes the electoral college system as it works today, let alone takes into account recent Supreme Court decisions affecting the selection process.

After Chapter 1 sets the scene for this review of the electoral college process and poses the question "Should the electoral college survive?" Chapter 2 steps back to look at why the electoral college was set up as it was. It also considers such questions as whether the Founders really were ambivalent about the selection process and reviews the historical precedents that have marked the existence of the electoral college itself. Chapter 3 then moves forward in time to review the presidential and vice-presidential selection procedure presently followed by the electoral college and to reveal the potential points of controversy in that procedure. An examination of the vital roles of the House of Representatives and the Senate (Chapter 4) and the courts (Chapter 5) in presidential selection follow, accompanied by diagnoses of the ills that chronically plague the selection process. Cures for these ills are prescribed in Chapter 6 within the confines of the notions of nonproportional and proportional representation.

Indeed, as these chapters reveal, several areas seem to cry out for reform such as establishing a new procedure for selecting members of the electoral college and modernizing the procedure for selecting a president in the House of Representatives. But there are reasons to hesitate before performing radical surgery on the system—by, for example, altogether abolishing the electoral college.

All this being said, it is only fair to point out that the political science literature abounds with proposals and counterproposals for reform. But the more one ponders these issues, the more the problems appear to be an infinite mathematical regress, with each tentative answer producing two more questions. Is it any wonder, then, that the matter of presidential selection proved among the most intractable confronting the drafters of the Constitution? And even more astounding, why is it that after a track record of two hundred years, the nation is no closer to consensus today than the Founders were back then? This is unfortunate. The nation has seen three major third-party challenges in twenty-five years—by George Wallace, John Anderson, and Perot—and unless the system is changed to remedy the problems, these issues will again be forced to the surface by another such challenge.

I could not have produced this book without the help of numerous people. Ginny Sloan gave me invaluable documents not readily available. Vik Amar, Akhil Reed Amar, Ann Bruner, Larry Berman, Lou Fisher, Floyd Feeney, Tom Franck, Bob Hillman, Mark Glennon, Bruce Jentleson, and Ginny Sloan were generous with comments on an earlier draft. My research assistant, Keltie

Jones, was a thoughtful critic. The University of California, Davis, Law School and the University of California, Davis, Washington Center provided helpful support. Berta Lewin's dexterity at word processing and graphics was superb. And Jeanne Ferris and Sabra Ledent at Congressional Quarterly Press were as patient and attentive editors as any author could want.

Michael J. Glennon
Davis, California

Chapter 1

The Electoral College:
An Institution for All Times?

Whatever the meaning of the term *democracy*, the Framers thought they could distinguish one from a republic. To them, democracy meant government without intermediaries—that is, plebiscitary government, with governmental decisions made directly by the people. The New England town meeting is the classic example of such a government. In contrast, a republic was thought to imply representation. Decisions were made not by the people themselves but by officials selected by the people. The Framers favored republicanism because it promised wiser government. James Madison, writing in *Federalist* No. 10, observed that republican reliance on representation permitted the government to "refine and enlarge the public views, by passing them through the medium of a chosen body of citizens." [1] Republics were governed by people selected for their civic virtue, who deliberated; democracies were ruled by the mob, which was uninformed, emotional, and manipulable. Alexander Hamilton believed that the "deliberative sense of the community should govern." Republicanism, he stressed, "does not require an unqualified complaisance to every sudden breeze of passion to every transient impulse which the public may receive from the arts of men who flatter their prejudices to betray their interests." [2] Contemporary political observer Garry Wills has noted the Framers' affinity for Rome rather than Greece, pointing out that "they thought of Athens as ruled by mobs." [3]

So it was no accident that the Framers provided for the selection of U.S. senators by state legislatures; assigned responsibility for treaty approval to the Senate (rather than the "people's branch," the House of Representatives); required, in Article IV, section 4, of the Constitution, the federal government to guarantee the

1

states a "Republican Form of Government"; and formed an interme-
diate body—the electoral college—to choose a president and vice
president.

Alexander Hamilton, perhaps the chief architect of the electoral
college, thoroughly distrusted popular democracy. He wrote in
Federalist No. 68 that the electoral college would ensure that a few
men of insight and reflection would select the ablest president. "A
small number of persons, selected by their fellow-citizens from the
general mass," he hoped, would act "under circumstances favorable
to deliberation." Hamilton believed that such a system would thus
select as president "characters pre-eminent for ability and virtue."
He considered civic agitation less likely if the public participation
were directed at choosing many rather than one; the objective of
tranquil detachment on the part of the electors counseled against one
large convention, which would "expose them to heats and ferments."

Expanding on this idea, Hamilton noted that a body already in
existence would pose the threat of dealmaking. But such a body as
the electoral college, chosen for one purpose, was less susceptible to
scheming. Thus, the potential bias of the most preeminent preexisting group, the Congress, was ruled out, as the Constitution
prohibited its members from participating in the electoral college.
Keeping Congress out of the process, Hamilton thought, would
ensure the independence of the presidency. If Congress were free to
choose the president, the chief executive might "be tempted to
sacrifice his duty" to please those who had chosen him.[5]

Hamilton may seem out-of-touch today. Over a period of two
centuries, as Louis Henkin has pointed out, the United States has
largely moved away from republicanism, becoming a democracy
"without conscious conversion."[6] It has moved, in Wills's terms,
toward Greece, away from Rome. The Senate is now elected directly
by the people; the House participates in approving many significant
international agreements; the "guarantee clause" has not been
enforced by the courts; and the electoral college has survived—but
barely.

Should the electoral college survive? The first step in answering
that question is to understand what function the electoral college was
intended to perform—why the presidential electoral system was set
up as it was. The next step is to examine how the electoral college
works, which entails understanding not only how it functions, but
also how it fits into the entire scheme of presidential selection. This

includes the so-called "contingent" election of a president by the House of Representatives. The principal objective of this book is to render that arcane procedure a bit more transparent. One can then ask whether the original rationale for the procedure continues to apply. If it does not, have new reasons emerged that support its retention? Just as Winston Churchill concluded about democracy, the electoral college system is probably the worst possible method of choosing a president—except for all the others.

NOTES

1. *The Federalist Papers,* with an introduction by Edward Mead Earle (New York: Robert B. Luce, 1976), 59.
2. *Federalist Papers,* 464.
3. Garry Wills, *Lincoln at Gettysburg: The Words that Remade America* (New York: Simon and Schuster, 1992), 42.
4. *Federalist Papers,* 441-442, 444.
5. Philip B. Kurland and Ralph Lerner, eds., *The Founders' Constitution,* Vol. 3 (Chicago: University of Chicago Press, 1987), 550-551.
6. Louis Henkin, *Constitutionalism, Democracy and Foreign Affairs* (New York: Columbia University Press, 1990), 12.

Chapter 2

Origins of the Electoral College

A lexander Hamilton managed to escape the constraints of modesty in publicly evaluating his creation, the electoral college. He wrote in 1788 in *Federalist* No. 68:

The mode of appointment of the chief magistrate of the United States is almost the only part of the system, of any consequence, which has escaped without severe censure, or which has received the slightest mark of approbation from its opponents. . . . I venture somewhat further . . . that if the manner of it be not perfect, it is at least excellent.[1]

Privately, however, Hamilton was less commendatory. He feared that use of the electoral college would lead inadvertently to the election of John Adams over George Washington, whom everyone assumed would and should be the first president. Less than a year later, Hamilton acknowledged the procedure's flaws in a letter to James Wilson. "Everybody is aware of that defect in the Constitution," he wrote, "which renders it possible that the man intended for Vice President may actually turn up President."[2] As described later in this chapter, this nearly occurred in the election of 1800.

Intent of the Framers

The Framers' "intent" is always problematic. No "official" records were kept beyond, of course, the text on which the Founders agreed. Their true intent, to the extent known, might well be said to be reflected only in the text that they produced. Although James Madison unofficially took notes at the Constitutional Convention, they were not published until forty years after the convention. Several other drafters also recorded their recollections, but it is not known whether such records are accurate or complete. Nor is it known how many delegates were present when the reported remarks were made, or whether those delegates agreed or disagreed with the reported comments. Finally, a strong case can be made that the real "Framers" of the Constitution were not the delegates to the Philadelphia convention at all but rather were the delegates to the state ratifying conventions. The latter actually voted on the Constitution.

The Philadelphia Agenda

At the Constitutional Convention, it seems that the Framers were ambivalent about how the president should be chosen. Originally, the choice of president was given to Congress. Then the convention decided that the president should be chosen by electors. Later consideration restored the choice to Congress. Toward the close of the convention, however, the matter was referred to a committee that recommended a procedure similar to the one ultimately adopted.[3] In moving from one alternative to another, the Framers expressed concerns about elements of the presidential selection process that reverberate to this day.

The Framers' ambivalence was generated, perhaps, by disagreement over two fundamental questions. First, in what theory of democracy should the presidential selection process be grounded? Would the objective of the system be to fill the position of president with the best person or—in the event the two were different—with the people's choice? Second, on what theory of federalism should that process be based? Would the system reflect differences in the states' populations, or would the states be considered equal sovereignties, with each casting one vote?

To resolve the issue of democratic theory in favor of the people's will suggests a plebiscitary process consisting simply of a direct popular election. But to resolve that issue strictly in favor of merit might militate in favor of a selection process removed from popular opinion. (The word *might* is used because of the elusiveness of the concept of *merit,* even in that day. Merit, defined broadly, might include popular support, and it could therefore be argued that the most meritorious candidate is the one with the greatest popular support.)

Resolving the issue of federalism to reflect population differences among the states requires some form of district-by-district representation, either in the electoral college or the House of Representatives. Resolving it in a manner reflecting state sovereignty, however, supports the establishment of a process in which each state casts one vote.

The Philadelphia Debate

The suggestion that the Framers were ambivalent in their responses to these issues can be put even more starkly: it is difficult to glean any unifying philosophy animating the presidential selection procedure embodied in the Constitution. Neither their remarks at the Constitutional Convention nor the constitutional text that emerged from those deliberations nor the records of the state-ratifying conventions give evidence of a coherent theoretical framework.

· Many delegates to the Constitutional Convention favored popular election of the president. They included James Madison, James Wilson, John Dickinson, Rufus King, Daniel Carroll, and Abraham Baldwin. Many others, however, had serious doubts about the capacity of the people to choose a chief executive wisely in a direct election. William Blackstone, whose 1765 *Commentaries* strongly impressed the Framers, wrote that "history and observation will inform us, that elections of every kind (in the present state of human nature) are too frequently brought about by influence, partiality, and artifice." [4] Elbridge Gerry feared the "ignorance of the people," [5] arguing that they were "too little informed of personal characters in large districts, and liable of deceptions" to act directly. [6] George Mason believed it "as unnatural to refer the choice of a proper character for chief Magistrate to the people, as it would, to refer a trial of colours to a blind man." [7] Oliver Ellsworth, Luther Martin, and Roger Sherman also opposed popular selection.

The doubts about the people's ability to choose a president led in turn to misgivings about the competence of the proposed electoral college. Hugh Williamson, for example, had "no great confidence" that the people would choose able electors. He worried that the electors "would not be the most respectable citizens [and] would be liable to undue influence." [8] Some delegates therefore preferred that Congress select the president. Charles Pinckney argued that because members of Congress would be "immediately interested in the laws made by themselves," they would be likely to select "a fit man to carry them properly into execution." [9] Roger Sherman also favored placing the choice in Congress to make the president "absolutely dependent on that body." [10]

But most in Philadelphia opposed congressional selection. Gerry believed that there would be "constant intrigue kept up for the appointment." Congress and the candidates would bargain with votes given by Congress in return for services promised by the president. [11] Robert Morris argued that the president should not be "the mere creature of the Legislature." He should be elected by the people at large, Morris contended, to avoid "the work of intrigue, of cabal, and of faction" stemming from congressional selection. [12] • Madison was one of the prime opponents of congressional selection. "An election by the Legislature," he wrote a year after the Philadelphia Convention, "not only tends to faction intrigue and corruption, but leaves the Executive under the influence of an improper obligation to that department. An election by the people at large, . . . or by Electors . . . , seems to be far preferable." [13]

Initial selection of a president by electors became then the chief remaining alternative. Madison believed that, because electors "would be chosen for the occasion, would meet at once and proceed immediately to an appointment, there would be very little opportunity for cabal, or corruption." [14] Like Rufus King, [15] Madison preferred that electors be chosen by district rather than by the state winner-take-all system. [16] Joseph Story summarized the thinking of many at the Constitutional Convention in his *Commentaries on the Constitution* in 1833: "[A] small number of persons selected by their fellow citizens from the general mass for this special object, would be most likely to possess the information, and discernment, and independence, essential for the proper discharge of the duty." [17]

Many years later, Professor Lucius Wilmerding asserted that "the mode adopted was considered by the Founding Fathers an equivalent to an election by the people." [18] He also observed that the electors "were never meant to choose the President but only to pronounce the votes of the people." [19] If the Framers evinced any intent, however, it was to the contrary. An 1826 Senate committee report concluded that the electors "have not answered the design of their institution. They are not the independent body and superior • characters which they were intended to be." [20] In *McPherson v. Blacker* (1892), the Supreme Court disagreed with Wilmerding's interpretation of the original intent (for more on this case and others dealing with the electoral college, see Chapter 3). [21] The Court said the Framers probably "supposed that the electors would exercise a reasonable independence and fair judgment in the selection of the Chief Executive." The Court went on to say that experience soon demonstrated that, regardless of the method of selection, electors simply registered the "will of the appointing power in respect of a particular candidate." The prevailing view was accurately stated by ·Justice John Harlan, concurring in *Williams v. Rhodes* (1968): "The College was created to permit the most knowledgeable members of the community to choose the executive of a nation whose continental dimensions were thought to preclude an informed choice ·by the citizenry at large." [22] Justice Robert Jackson stated the matter even more forcefully: "No one faithful to our history can deny that the plan originally contemplated, what is implicit in its text, that electors would be free agents, to exercise an independent and nonpartisan judgment as to the men best qualified for the Nation's highest offices." [23]

The Philadelphia Results

In drafting the presidential selection procedure set out in Article II of the Constitution (see Appendix A), the Framers reached compromises in applying the concepts of democracy and federalism. The electoral college was based on the premise of selection by a few. Its architects rejected the notion of popular sovereignty. If the electoral college were to deadlock, however, the election would go to the House of Representatives, where the underlying theories reversed. There the selection would be made by individuals elected directly by the people, as opposed to the electoral college, where electors could have been chosen by state authorities with no reference to majority preference. And state sovereignty would prevail in the House since each state would there cast one vote, regardless of size.

Thus, the text of the Constitution itself, like the Philadelphia debate that produced it, discloses an inability or unwillingness on the part of the Framers to settle on a philosophically coherent theory. "There cannot be a greater political solecism," said Rep. George McDuffie (D-S.C.) in 1826, "than that which is involved in the idea of commencing the election of the President upon one principle, and ending it according to another." He continued:

If the popular principle is the true principle of this election, as indicated by the Constitution itself, nothing can be more absurd than to abandon it

When No Majority Rules

entirely as soon as the People, at the first effort, fail to give a majority of votes for one candidate. It looks like punishing the People, by forfeiture, for not being more unanimous.[24]

Evolution of the Electoral College

In *Williams v. Rhodes* Justice Harlan recalled Madison's belief that the prevailing view at the time the Constitution was adopted was that electors would be selected district by district. Nonetheless, Harlan observed that a significant group at the convention contemplated that some states would prefer other methods of choosing electors. To accommodate this group, the convention agreed to give state legislatures leeway in prescribing the method of selection. Harlan also noted that during the first four decades of the Republic, the states adopted several methods for selecting electors, including appointment "by the legislature itself, by the general electorate on an at-large and district-by-district basis, partly by the legislature and partly by the people, by the legislature from a list of candidates selected by the people, and in other ways." [25]

State Legislatures Empowered to
Select a Method for Choosing Electors

As noted, the convention unfortunately settled on a presidential selection system lacking a unified theoretical rationale. Even at the electoral college stage, it did not set forth a clear philosophy of democracy. As for the all-important question of how the electors were to be chosen, the convention demurred, passing that question on to the states for a decision. Each state was permitted to appoint electors "in such manner as the legislature thereof may direct." [26] Even Congress was thus precluded from guiding the procedure's evolution. Charles Pinckney, looking back in 1800, was emphatic: "Nothing was more clear . . . than that Congress had no right to meddle with [the electoral college] at all; as the whole was entrusted to the State Legislatures, they must make provisions for all questions arising on the occasion." [27] By the 1830s, state legislatures had stopped choosing electors but the constitutionality of the practice was still strongly defended. As late as 1874, a Senate committee report said:

The appointment of these electors is thus placed absolutely and wholly with the legislatures of the several States. They may be chosen by the legislature, or the legislature may provide that they shall be elected by the people of the State at large, or in districts, as are members of Congress, which was the case formerly in many States; and it is, no doubt, competent for the legislature to authorize the governor, or the Supreme Court of the State, or any other agent of its will, to appoint these electors. This power is conferred upon the legislatures of the States by the Constitution of the United States, and cannot be taken from them or modified by their State constitutions any more than can their power to elect Senators of the United States. Whatever provisions may be made by statute, or by the state constitution, to choose electors by the people, there is no doubt of the right of the legislature to resume the power at any time, for it can neither be taken away nor abdicated.[28]

The Supreme Court implicitly confirmed the permissibility of a state legislature picking electors in 1892, when the constitutionality ·of the district system was challenged in *McPherson v. Blacker*.[29] The argument against the system was grounded in part in history: the district system, it was contended, while "not obnoxious to the Constitution in its original object and purpose," had in effect become "obnoxious to that plan as it was practically and ultimately developed, and as it has now for sixty years actually existed." The challengers argued that the Court should abandon the electoral college as it existed at the time despite a century of practical experience and development. Their reasoning was that the original design was obsolete.

But the Court rejected the notion that this "evolution" had rendered the district system unconstitutional. It said that it could find "no reason for holding that the power confided to the States by the Constitution has ceased to exist because the operation of the system has not fully realized the hopes of those by whom it was created." It also rejected the notion that flexibility in constitutional interpretation permitted de facto judicial amendment.

Although it recognized that the district system had been long abandoned, the Court nonetheless concluded that states maintained the power to employ it. State legislatures, it pointed out, possess "plenary authority to direct the manner of appointment" of electors. In fact, a state legislature can itself appoint electors by joint ballot or concurrence of the two houses, or similar methods if it so desires. Based on this reasoning, the Court concluded that it would be hard to imagine why a legislature could choose the "general ticket" system but not the district system.

From the language of this opinion, one might think that the discretion accorded state legislatures in fashioning rules for the selection of presidential electors—even archaic rules—is seemingly unbridled. Wilmerding believed that under the Constitution, states can select any method of picking electors. He wrote that a state legislature may permit the choice to be made by the people, by both houses of the legislature, by one house, by a legislative committee, or by the governor. Quoting Michael Hoffman, a Democratic representative of New York in 1826, he added that there is nothing to prevent the legislature from vesting that power "in a board of Bank directors—a turnpike corporation—or a synagogue. . . . Any mode, whether suggested by the sense of equity and fair play or by the ferocity of faction, is permissible." [30] This view vastly overstates legislative discretion, however. The Supreme Court, as discussed in the next chapter, has made it clear that not every mode of selection is permissible.

Emergence of the General Ticket System

• Three modes of electoral selection were actually adopted by state legislatures: (1) the legislative system, in which electors were selected by state legislatures; (2) the district system, in which electors were selected by the people in their congressional districts; and (3) the general ticket, or winner-take-all, system, in which every voter voted for every elector to which the state was entitled. Observers decried the instability, malleability, and lack of uniformity of these procedures. Reforms were proposed regularly, but none was adopted because the political parties that controlled the electoral machinery would have faced greater competition.

Another reason the reform movement failed was that the electoral selection procedure gradually became uniform. The winner-take-all, general ticket system ultimately emerged as the dominant model. The legislative system increasingly was seen as corrupt, entailing too much bargaining and too many promises and payoffs. Apparently, the controlling political parties believed they could retain their power more legitimately through the seeming democracy of the general ticket system. The political parties rejected the district system because it fostered the emergence of independent candidacies and third parties. Today, Maine and Nebraska are the only states that continue to employ the district system. In 1992, Florida considered adopting the district system, but it was rejected because state political officials gradually concluded that, in relation to other states that had adopted the general ticket system, Florida would receive less attention in presidential campaigns if its electoral votes were split.

The emergence of the general ticket system was outlined by the Supreme Court in *McPherson v. Blacker* (1892):

At the first presidential election the appointment of electors was made by the legislatures of Connecticut, Delaware, Georgia, New Jersey and South Carolina. Pennsylvania . . . provided for the election of electors on a general ticket. . . .

Fifteen States participated in the second presidential election, in nine of which electors were chosen by the legislatures. . . .

Sixteen States took part in the third presidential election. . . . In nine States the electors were appointed by the legislatures. . . .

In 1824 the electors were chosen by popular vote . . . in all the States [but six,] where they were still chosen by the legislature.[31]

By 1832, only South Carolina continued to choose electors by its legislature, and it continued to do so until 1860. Florida, however, adopted this method of selection in 1868, as did Colorado, in 1876.

With the spread of the general ticket system, electors began to merely rubber-stamp the results of the popular election—something not, of course, foreseen by the Framers. As early as 1816, Rufus King could observe that the "election of a President of the United States is no longer that process that the Constitution contemplated."[32] In 1833, Joseph Story opined in his *Commentaries:*

[I]n no respect have the enlarged and liberal views of the framers of the constitution, and the expectations of the public when it was adopted, been so completely frustrated. . . . It is notorious, that the electors are not chosen wholly with reference to particular candidates, and are silently pledged to vote for them. Nay, upon some occasions the electors publicly pledge themselves to vote for a particular person; and thus, in effect, the whole foundation of the system so elaborately constructed, is subverted. . . . So, that nothing is left to the electors after their choice, but to register votes, which are already pledged. . . .[33]

Wilmerding aptly described contemporary electors as "mere mandarin toys that nod when they are set in motion."[34]

Historical Precedents: An Overview

In three elections—1800, 1824, and 1876—the mandarin toys nodded in unwanted directions.

Election of 1800

Under the original Constitution, electors did not vote separately for president and vice president as they do today. They simply cast two votes for president. The runner-up became vice president. Had elections remained the nonpartisan process that the Framers had envisioned, this procedure might have worked. No problems arose in the elections of 1789 and 1792, even though the Federalist and Democratic-Republican parties had begun to coalesce. (The famous "botany expedition" of James Madison and Thomas Jefferson to New York—which was, in fact, an organizational mission to lay the groundwork for the Democratic-Republican party—occurred during George Washington's first term, in 1791.) Perhaps this early electoral unanimity existed because, despite electors' philosophical differences, they joined unquestioningly in support of Washington.

That unanimity broke down when Washington retired from the scene, causing the system's collapse. In 1796, Thomas Jefferson, a Democratic Republican, ran against Vice President John Adams, a Federalist. Jefferson finished second in the electoral college vote and was therefore elected vice president, serving under his opponent, President Adams.

In 1800, the Democratic-Republican party again ran Jefferson as its presidential candidate and Aaron Burr as its vice-presidential candidate. An equal number of the Democratic-Republican electors voted for both Jefferson and Burr, thus throwing the election into the House of Representatives. It took thirty-six ballots, cast between February 11 and February 17, before Jefferson received a majority of the votes. Burr, finishing second, became vice president.

Obviously, the system had to be changed. If all electors from the same party voted for the same two individuals, a tie would result, throwing the election into the House and increasing the risk of "inversion"—selection as president of the individual intended to be vice president. The result was the Twelfth Amendment, which Congress initiated immediately after the 1800 election and which became part of the Constitution in 1804 (see Appendix A). The Supreme Court described its purpose in *Ray v. Blair* (1952).[35] Under the original Constitution, the Court explained, the electors of each state did not vote separately for president and vice president; rather, they voted for two persons, without specifying whether the vote was for president or vice president. If all the electors of the predominant party voted for the same two men, the election resulted in a tie. In such cases, the election would be thrown into the House, which might or might not be sympathetic to the same party. During the John Adams administration, the president and vice president hailed from different parties, "a situation," the Court said, "which could not commend itself either to the Nation or to most political theorists." It continued:

The situation was manifestly intolerable. Accordingly the Twelfth Amendment was adopted, permitting the electors to vote separately for presidential and vice-presidential candidates. Under this procedure, the party electors could vote the regular party ticket without throwing the election into the House. Electors could be chosen to vote for the party candidates for both offices, and the electors could carry out the desires of the people, without confronting the obstacles which confounded the elections of 1796 and 1800.[36]

Election of 1824

The election of 1824 was the one time after the adoption of the Twelfth Amendment that the electoral college deadlocked and an election was thrown into the House of Representatives. Five candidates ran in the 1824 election: John C. Calhoun, William H. Crawford, John Quincy Adams, Henry Clay, and Andrew Jackson. Jackson won a plurality of the popular vote cast, 42.4 percent. Adams finished second, with 31.9 percent; Clay, third, with 13.0 percent; and Crawford fourth, also with 13.0 percent. (In six states the legislatures selected presidential electors; no popular election was held.)

At the time, a majority of electoral votes was 131. Jackson received 99, Adams 84, and Crawford 41. The Twelfth Amendment required that the House decide the election since no candidate received a majority of the electoral votes.

Meeting in January 1825, the House proceeded to vote state by state. Under rules adopted by the House, each state's vote was determined by a majority of that state's representatives. If a candidate did not win a majority, the state was not permitted to vote. Adams won on the first ballot—even though he had received fewer popular votes than Jackson (108,740 for Adams and 153,544 for Jackson). Adams's victory, it was claimed, was the result of a deal with Clay, who, as Speaker of the House, was a most useful ally. After the election, Adams appointed Clay secretary of state. Four years later, Andrew Jackson ran a populist campaign against this "corrupt bargain" and won an overwhelming victory.

Election of 1876

The election of 1876 did not go to the House. It turned on a dispute concerning the validity of votes cast in the electoral college. The controversy was decided by an electoral commission, established by Congress with the requirement that each commission decision be approved by both the House and Senate.

Two major-party candidates ran for president in 1876: Samuel Tilden, a Democrat, and Rutherford B. Hayes, a Republican. Tilden, the governor of New York, won 50.9 percent of the popular vote to Hayes's 47.9 percent. In the electoral college, however, the results were much closer.

At the time, a candidate needed 185 votes to win a majority in the electoral college. Hayes received the required number, but the Democrats challenged one of his electoral votes, leaving him with only 184. Republican challenges to nineteen Tilden electoral votes in three states left Tilden with 165.

This was not the first time that votes in the electoral college had been challenged. Massachusetts's votes had been challenged in 1809, Indiana's in 1817, and Missouri's in 1820. But in each instance, Congress rejected the challenge. Thus, the precedent was established that Congress would not inquire into the certification of the validity of electoral votes by state officials.[37]

The Constitution, now as then, is silent on the procedures for determining the validity of electoral votes, and after the 1876 election the Republican-controlled House was unable to agree upon a compromise procedure with the Democratic-controlled Senate. Instead, the two houses agreed to set up an electoral commission, consisting of five senators, five representatives, and five justices of the Supreme Court. It was thought at the outset that the commission would be split seven to seven, with one of the Supreme Court justices—an independent—casting the tie-breaking vote. That justice became ineligible upon election to the Senate, however, and was replaced by another justice—Joseph Bradley—who (to the Democrats' surprise and chagrin) voted regularly with the Republicans. The commission awarded all twenty disputed electoral votes to Hayes, who therefore won by one electoral vote—after losing the popular vote.

But the battle was not over. Under the law establishing the commission, this outcome was not final until both houses of Congress had voted and at least one had approved the result. The Senate approved, but an effort emerged in the House to delay its vote beyond inauguration day. Fewer than twenty-four hours before Hayes was to receive the oath of office, the filibuster in the House collapsed, and Hayes was inaugurated president. Meanwhile, Justice Bradley was placed under armed guard because of threats on his life, and Hayes was the object of an assassination attempt.

In response to this debacle, Congress in 1887 enacted the Electoral Count Act. The act makes the states the initial judge of the validity of their electoral votes but subjects each electoral vote to possible disapproval by Congress by concurrent resolution, that is, a resolution adopted by both houses but not presented to the president for a possible veto. A modern version of this procedure is set forth in the U.S. Code, Title 3, section 15 (see Appendix B).

As is discussed in the next chapter, this division of authority between the states and Congress has created as many problems as it has solved, for the congressional power to "count" electoral votes inevitably overlaps with the power of the states to determine their validity at the outset.

NOTES

1. Philip B. Kurland and Ralph Ferner, eds., *The Founders' Constitution*, Vol. 3 (Chicago: University of Chicago Press, 1987), 550.
2. Ibid., 552.
3. Ibid., 555-558.
4. Ibid., 535.
5. Ibid., 542.
6. Ibid., 536.
7. Ibid., 538.
8. Ibid.
9. Ibid., 537.
10. Ibid., 536.
11. Ibid.
12. Ibid., 537.
13. Ibid., 551.
14. Ibid., 541.
15. Ibid., 555.
16. Ibid., 557.
17. Ibid., 588.
18. Lucius Wilmerding, Jr., *The Electoral College* (New Brunswick, N.J.: Rutgers University Press, 1958), 171.
19. Ibid., 174.

20. Senate Select Committee on Amendments to the Constitution, *Report on the Several Resolutions Proposing Amendments to the Constitution, as Regards the Election of President and Vice President of the United States,* S. Rept. 22, 19th Cong., 1st sess., 1826, 4.
21. *McPherson v. Blacker,* 146 U.S. 1 (1892).
22. *Williams v. Rhodes,* 393 U.S. 23 (1968) at 43-44.
23. *Ray v. Blair,* 343 U.S. 214 (1952) at 232.
24. Wilmerding, *Electoral College,* 185.
25. *Williams v. Rhodes,* 393 U.S. 23 (1968) at 44-45, 45 n. 6.
26. U.S. Constitution, Article II, section 1, clause 2.
27. Kurland and Lerner, *Founders' Constitution,* 553.
28. Senate Committee on Privileges and Elections, *Report on the Most Practicable Mode of Electing the President and Vice President,* S. Rept. 395, 43d Cong., 1st sess., 1874, 9, quoted in *McPherson v. Blacker,* 146 U.S. 1 (1892) at 34-35.
29. *McPherson v. Blacker,* 146 U.S. 1 (1892) at counsel statements 36, 25.
30. Wilmerding, *Electoral College,* 42-43.
31. *McPherson v. Blacker,* 146 U.S. 1 (1892) at 29-31.
32. Kurland and Lerner, *Founders' Constitution,* 555.
33. Ibid., 559.
34. Wilmerding, *Electoral College,* xi.
35. *Ray v. Blair,* 343 U.S. 214 (1952) at 225.
36. Ibid.
37. Wallace S. Sayre and Judith H. Parris, *Voting for President* (Washington, D.C.: Brookings, 1970), 29.

Chapter 3

The Electoral College Today

M ost voters vote under an illusion. They believe that they are voting directly for a president and vice president. They are not aware that when they cast their ballots for president and vice president, they are voting not for those officials but rather for the people, so-called electors, who will cast their votes for president and vice president (see Figure 3-1). In some states, the candidates for elector are actually listed on the November ballot. In most, they are not.

Presidential Election Procedure

In December, following the general election, the electors meet in the states from which they were selected. The term *electoral college* is in this sense a misnomer; there is no collective gathering of the kind that occurs when, say, the College of Cardinals selects a pope. Each state is allotted a number of electors equal to the number of its representatives and senators (two) in Congress. Including the three electors representing the District of Columbia, the electoral college has, then, 538 members. The electors normally cast their ballots for the presidential and vice-presidential candidates to whom they are pledged. If a presidential candidate receives a majority of the electoral vote (270), that candidate is elected president. If a candidate for vice president receives a majority of the electoral vote, that candidate is elected vice president. If no presidential candidate receives a majority of the electoral vote, the House of Representatives chooses a president. Likewise, if no vice-presidential candidate receives a majority of the vote, the Senate chooses a vice president. In undertaking these procedures, the House and Senate are guided by

When No Majority Rules

FIGURE 3-1
How Presidents and Vice Presidents Are Chosen

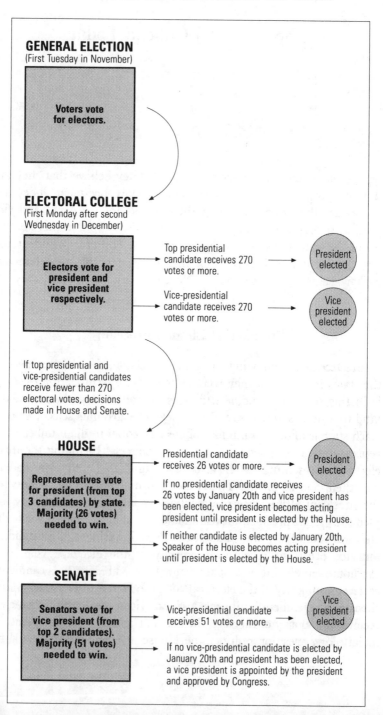

GENERAL ELECTION
(First Tuesday in November)

Voters vote for electors.

ELECTORAL COLLEGE
(First Monday after second Wednesday in December)

Electors vote for president and vice president respectively.

Top presidential candidate receives 270 votes or more. → President elected

Vice-presidential candidate receives 270 votes or more. → Vice president elected

If top presidential and vice-presidential candidates receive fewer than 270 electoral votes, decisions made in House and Senate.

HOUSE

Representatives vote for president (from top 3 candidates) by state. Majority (26 votes) needed to win.

Presidential candidate receives 26 votes or more. → President elected

If no presidential candidate receives 26 votes by January 20th and vice president has been elected, vice president becomes acting president until president is elected by the House.

If neither candidate is elected by January 20th, Speaker of the House becomes acting president until president is elected by the House.

SENATE

Senators vote for vice president (from top 2 candidates). Majority (51 votes) needed to win.

Vice-presidential candidate receives 51 votes or more. → Vice president elected

If no vice-presidential candidate is elected by January 20th and president has been elected, a vice president is appointed by the president and approved by Congress.

the Twelfth Amendment to the U.S. Constitution (Appendix A) and U.S. Title 3 of the Code (see Appendix B).

The new House of Representatives, convening in January, chooses from the top three presidential candidates in the electoral college vote. Each state delegation has one vote (the District of Columbia has none). If a candidate receives a majority of the House vote (26), that candidate is deemed to have been elected president. In the event no presidential candidate receives a majority of the House vote by January 20, inauguration day, then under the Twentieth Amendment the vice president-elect "shall act as President until a President shall have qualified."

If no vice president is chosen by the electoral college, the new Senate, convening in January, chooses from among the top two vice-presidential candidates in the electoral college vote. If a candidate receives a majority of the Senate vote (51), that candidate is deemed to have been elected vice president. If the House selects a president but the Senate fails to select a vice president by January 20, then, under the Twenty-fifth Amendment, a vice president is appointed by the president and approved by Congress.

If neither the House nor the Senate has selected a president or vice president by January 20, then under the Twentieth Amendment (Appendix A) and the Presidential Succession Act of 1947 (see Appendix B) the Speaker of the House becomes acting president. The Speaker remains in office until the House selects a president. If the Speaker is unable to serve, then the president pro tempore of the Senate acts as President. If both are unable to serve, then the person next in line—the secretary of state—acts as president.

The United States has never had an "acting" president. Indeed, it is hard to imagine a person serving as president and then being compelled to leave office when one with greater entitlement appears on the scene. But that is the system. The vice president, Speaker of the House, or whoever acts as president does so only until the proper individual qualifies. This can occur at any time during the four-year presidential term. At that point, the vice president or Speaker vacates the office of President—actually, ceases to "act" as president; neither has ever actually been president—and the president is sworn in.

The positions of Speaker of the House and president pro tempore of the Senate can be filled with individuals other than those holding the office at the time it becomes clear that one of those persons will be called on to act as president. In the past, it has not always been true that the person occupying each position would have been the choice of the House or Senate to act as president had circumstances so required.

Indeed, it is not altogether clear that the Speaker must be a member of the House or that the president pro tempore of the Senate must be a member of the Senate. Article I, section 2, clause 4, of the Constitution provides that the "House of Representatives shall chuse their Speaker and other Officers"; Article I, section 3, clause 5, provides that the "Senate shall chuse their other Officers, and also a President pro tempore, in the Absence of the Vice President, or when he shall exercise the Office of President of the United States." Neither provision indicates that the Speaker, president pro tempore, or any officer must be a member of the body over which they will preside. Under the Constitution, the vice president is president of the Senate even though never elected to the Senate; the sergeant-at-arms of each body is considered an officer of that body, as is the doorkeeper of the House and the secretary of the Senate. None is a member.

It is worth noting, however, that this is not the way federal law construes the Constitution. The Presidential Succession Act permits the Speaker to act as president only "upon his resignation as Speaker and as Representative in Congress." Similarly, the president pro tempore of the Senate may act as president only "upon his resignation as President pro tempore and as Senator." Congress, in enacting these succession provisions, thus seems to have assumed that these two officers would in fact be members of the House and Senate.

Electors

Selection

Because under the Twelfth Amendment (Appendix A) each state is allocated a number of electoral votes equal to its total number of senators and representatives, no state has fewer than three electoral votes—this is in fact the number cast by Alaska, Montana, and Vermont. California, in contrast, has fifty-four electoral votes. Although it has no voting representatives in Congress, the District of Columbia by law has three electors. The electoral college consists, then, of fifty-one smaller "colleges," which altogether have 538 members.

As discussed in Chapter 2, all states but Maine and Nebraska have now adopted the winner-take-all system. Under this system, all of the state's electoral votes go to the candidate who wins the largest popular vote in the November election, even though it may be only a plurality rather than a majority. Maine and Nebraska, however, allot electoral votes congressional district by congressional district, with the winner of the statewide popular vote receiving the two remaining electoral votes.

The predominant method of selecting the individual who will serve as elector is the state party convention. As of 1988 thirty-seven states nominated their presidential and vice-presidential electors at state party conventions (see Table 3-1). The party's central committee makes the choice in eleven states and the District of Columbia. The two remaining states leave it to the parties to choose a method of selection.

The persons chosen by the parties are not actual electors—at least, not yet. First, they must win election. As described above, all states now choose electors in the direct popular election held in November.

Yet, in that election many voters do not realize that they are in reality voting for electors rather than for president and vice president. Little wonder they might be confused: forty-two states do not print the names of the electors on the ballot. All the voters see is the name of the party's nominees for president and vice president. In those forty-two states, a voter is deemed to have voted for the party's electors when the voter selected the names of the presidential and vice-presidential candidates. Some states, such as Illinois,[1] state this explicitly; others, such as California,[2] imply it.

Qualifications

• Only one constitutional restriction limits who may serve as an elector: Article II, section 1, clause 2, provides that "no Senator or Representative, or Person holding an Office of Trust or Profit under the United States, shall be appointed an Elector." Thus, a person elected to Congress but not yet sworn in may serve as an elector; that person is not yet a senator or representative. What constitutes an office of trust or profit is not clear. In *Buckley v. Valeo* (1976),[3] the Supreme Court said: "We think [that] any appointee exercising significant authority pursuant to the laws of the United States is an Officer of the United States. . . ." So it would seem that at least some

TABLE 3-1

Methods of Selecting Electors, by State

State political party convention	Political party's central committee	Political party
Alabama	California	Arizona
Alaska	Florida	Maryland
Arkansas	Louisiana	
Colorado	Massachusetts	
Connecticut	Missouri	
Delaware	Montana	
Georgia	New Jersey	
Hawaii	New York	
Idaho	Pennsylvania	
Illinois	South Carolina	
Indiana	Tennessee	
Iowa	District of Columbia	
Kansas		
Kentucky		
Maine		
Michigan		
Minnesota		
Mississippi		
Nebraska		
Nevada		
New Hampshire		
New Mexico		
North Carolina		
North Dakota		
Ohio		
Oklahoma		
Oregon		
Rhode Island		
South Dakota		
Texas		
Utah		
Vermont		
Virginia		
Washington		
West Virginia		
Wisconsin		
Wyoming		

officials of the executive branch—those holding an office of "trust or profit"—are also precluded from serving as electors.

When Electors Are Appointed

The Constitution does not set a date for the appointment of electors. Federal law requires the electors' appointment on the first Tuesday after the first Monday in November, the day on which the popular election is held. Notwithstanding the broad power given states over the appointment of electors, Congress has removed the issue of timing from state hands, and apparently no state has contested Congress's power to do so.

Procedure in the Electoral College

On the fundamental elements of electoral college procedure, the law is clear, having been set out in Article I of the Constitution (Appendix A) and Title 3 of the U.S. Code (Appendix B).

When and Where Electors Meet

The Constitution does not specify when electors meet. This date too is prescribed by federal law, which sets it at the first Monday after the second Wednesday in December.

Where electors meet is addressed by the Constitution: the Twelfth Amendment provides that electors "shall meet in their respective states." Most states provide by law that the meeting will occur in the state capital. As a consequence, the electoral college is, again, not a "college" at all in the sense implied. At no time do all its members meet jointly.

Inability of an Appointed Elector to Serve

Federal statutory law allows states to provide by law for the filling of any vacancy that may occur. Not all do so; among those that do, a number (such as Connecticut⁴) provide that the vacancy be filled by a vote of the other electors.

Voting Procedure

Federal statutory law governs the process by which electoral votes are cast and counted. It provides, first, that the electors make and sign six certificates listing their choices for president and vice president and then seal the certificates. The electors are then required to send one of the certificates to the president of the U.S. Senate, who is also the vice president of the United States. On January 6, the House of Representatives and the Senate meet together in the chamber of the House of Representatives, and the votes are counted by four tellers, two appointed by each body. Finally, the vice president announces the results.

Points of Potential Controversy in the Electoral College

The voting process in the electoral college, laid out step by step, seems straightforward enough. But at a number of stages, controversy can arise. In some instances, those disputes have been anticipated, and solutions are spelled out in law. But in other instances, new disputes may emerge, presenting questions of first impression. A brief look at the potential trouble spots in the process will highlight these issues.

State-Imposed Barriers to the Appointment of Electors

The Constitution, again, sets forth only one qualification for appointment as an elector: it excludes any "Senator or Representative, or Person holding an Office of Trust or Profit under the United States. . . ." It has been argued that no further limitations are permissible. The argument implies that even traditional factors such as age or period of residency within the state may not be taken into account. In *Powell v. McCormack* (1969,)[5] it was contended that the House of Representatives could impose qualifications for membership in the House beyond those imposed by the Constitution. The Supreme Court rejected the argument, holding that the House was limited to applying the membership criteria explicitly set forth in the Constitution. Electors may be different from members of Congress in that the Constitution does, after all, give the state legislatures broad power to select electors. It provides that "[e]ach State shall appoint, in such manner as the Legislature thereof may direct, a Number of Electors." This power seems no broader than that at issue in *Powell*, however, where the House of Representatives argued that it was granted plenary power by the constitutional provision authorizing it—and only it—to "be the judge of the . . . qualifications of its own members."[6] So perhaps a state seeking to add qualifications for the office of elector would be on no firmer footing than was the House in seeking to add qualifications for the office of U.S. representative.

The view that state discretion cannot be circumscribed derives in part from the sweeping language of the Supreme Court in the case of *McPherson v. Blacker* (1892) (see Appendix C). The Court in that case was confronted with the argument that state power to appoint electors had been limited by the adoption of the Fourteenth and Fifteenth amendments. The Court said that "from the formation of the government until now the practical construction of the clause [Article II, section 1, clause 2] has conceded plenary power to the state legislatures in the matter of the appointment of electors." It continued:

The Constitution does not provide that the appointment of electors shall be by popular vote, nor that the electors shall be voted for upon a general ticket, nor that the majority of those who exercise the elective franchise can alone choose the electors. It recognizes that the people act through their representatives in the legislature, and leaves it to the legislature exclusively to define the method of effecting the object. . . .

In short, the appointment and mode of appointment of electors belong exclusively to the States under the Constitution of the United States.[7]

Pursuant to this power to determine the "mode of appointment," many states, such as Connecticut, require the filing of a petition (typically signed by 1 percent of the number of persons voting in the previous election) when a candidate applies to be listed on the election ballot.[8]

Like other plenary powers, however, those residing within state legislatures to select the method of appointment of electors are not unlimited. The Court in fact recognized limits in *McPherson* in assessing whether the challenged Michigan statute violated other constitutional limits. (It held that it did not.) In a 1968 case, the Court left no doubt that state legislatures are, indeed, constrained by other constitutional provisions in the electoral procedures they can adopt. *Williams v. Rhodes* (1968) involved a challenge to a series of Ohio statutes that the Court said, "made it virtually impossible for a new political party, even though it has hundreds of thousands of members, or an old party, which has a very small number of members, to be placed on the state ballot to choose electors pledged to particular candidates for the Presidency and Vice Presidency of the United States" (see Appendix C).[9] The statute went even further with respect to independent candidates for elector: it barred them completely from getting on the ballot. Ohio claimed the power to keep minority parties and independent candidates off the ballot under Article II, section 1, of the Constitution.

In this case, the Supreme Court began by confirming what was implicit in *McPherson*—that the Constitution limits state power to constrict the selection of electors. In a plurality opinion written by Justice Hugo Black and joined by three other justices, it noted that Ohio had contended that it had absolute power to put any burdens it pleased on the selection of electors. This power, Ohio argued, flowed from Article II, section 1, of the Constitution, which provides that "[e]ach State shall appoint, in such Manner as the Legislature thereof may direct, a Number of Electors" to choose a president and vice president.

The Court rejected the argument. It observed that "the Constitution is filled with provisions that grant Congress or the States specific power to legislate in certain areas," but all of these granted powers are subject to other constitutional limitations, such as the Fifth Amendment privilege against self-incrimination. The Court held that no state can pass a law regulating elections that violates the Fourteenth Amendment's command that "[n]o State shall . . . deny to any person . . . the equal protection of the laws." The Ohio statutes, the Court found, burdened two different rights: first, the right of individuals to associate for the advancement of political beliefs and, second, the right of qualified voters, regardless of their political persuasion, to cast their votes effectively. The Court concluded with a ringing reference to the right to vote: "No right is more precious in a free country than that of having a voice in the election of those who make the laws under which, as good citizens, we must live. Other rights, even the most basic, are illusory if the right to vote is undermined."

But there is a problem in this reasoning: how does a person have a "right" to vote for electors for president and vice president if a state legislature has the right—upheld by the Court in *McPherson v. Blacker* (1892)[10]—to deny voters that right? It will be recalled that the Court said in *McPherson* that "we can perceive no reason for holding that the power confided to the States by the Constitution has ceased to exist because the operation of the system has not fully realized the hopes of those by whom it was created." Long after the founding of the Republic, state legislatures persisted in selecting electors themselves. As Justice Potter Stewart said in his dissenting opinion in *Williams*,[11] "A State is perfectly free under the Constitution to provide for the selection of its presidential electors by the legislature itself. Such a process of appointment was in fact utilized by several States throughout our early history, and by one State, Colorado, as late as 1876." The *McPherson* opinion, cited by Justice Stewart, outlined state practice in some detail. Nothing in the *Williams* opinion suggests any intent to overrule *McPherson* or otherwise preclude state legislatures from limiting or denying altogether the popular franchise in presidential elections. "[T]here is," Justice Stewart wrote in *Williams,* "no constitutional right to vote for presidential electors."

This proposition seems startling, particularly in light of the Twenty-fourth Amendment. In section 1, it provides:

The right of citizens of the United States to vote in any primary or other election for President or Vice President, for electors for President or Vice President, or for Senator or Representative in Congress, shall not be denied or abridged by the United States or any State by reason of failure to pay any poll tax or other tax.

Justice Stewart construed this merely as precluding a poll tax where a state provides for the selection of electors at polls—not as *requiring* that a state provide for the selection of electors at polls. There is nothing explicit in the amendment to suggest an intent to override or otherwise narrow the application of Article II, section 1, of the Constitution, which provides that "[e]ach State shall appoint, in such Manner as the Legislature thereof may direct, a Number of Electors" to choose a president and vice president. Yet it is hard to imagine the Court today upholding a system of legislative or gubernatorial appointment of electors; voting for president simply has become too ingrained in the national political culture to be abolished at this late date.

The Court's plurality opinion ignored these issues, although they were implicitly recognized by the two additional members of the Court who joined in the conclusion that the Ohio statutes were unconstitutional. One, Justice William O. Douglas, wrote that it was unnecessary to decide "whether States may select [electors] through appointment rather than by popular vote, or whether there is a constitutional right to vote for them." In this case, Ohio had already provided that its electors would be chosen by popular vote. Having done so, Ohio could not encumber that right with the kinds of conditions it imposed. The Court found that the First Amendment right of association prohibited such state-imposed burdens.

The other justice filing a concurring opinion, John Harlan, rested the result on that same associational right. He addressed the issue directly: "The particular method by which presidential electors are chosen is not of decisive importance to a solution of the constitutional problem before us." Political groups have the right to place their presidential candidates before whatever body has the power to make the state's selection of electors. He acknowledged that Ohio could "place the power of Electoral selection beyond the control of the general electorate" but that due process requirements would still apply. "Political groups have a right to be heard," he wrote, before any state institution to which the decision is entrusted.

However this conundrum is resolved, clearly a state does not have unlimited power to prescribe the selection of presidential electors in any manner it may choose. The words of Justices Harlan and Stewart notwithstanding, it is hard to believe that the Court would today uphold the right of a state legislature to choose electors in a manner other than a popular vote. If it can, other constitutional guarantees surely must be respected.

Disputes over Constitutional Exclusion

As discussed earlier, the meaning of the Constitution's prohibition against electors holding an "Office of Trust or Profit under the United States" is unclear. Broadly construed, it could be taken to exclude any person holding a position of employment with the federal government, including members of the armed forces and all other persons who receive compensation from the United States at the time of their appointment as an elector. This interpretation seems too broad, however. A more sensible construction would limit the exclusion to a certain category of federal officials since the word "Office" is modified by "Trust or Profit," implying that the limitation does not apply to every office. The scope of that category is uncertain, but it would seem reasonably limited to high-ranking federal officials who exercise significant policy-making authority.

One reason for so construing the exclusion is its similarity to Article I, section 6, clause 2, which prohibits any member of Congress from "holding any office under the United States" during his or her tenure in Congress. The Supreme Court has declined to define the breadth of that limitation, but it has been suggested that the purpose was to preclude any semblance of a parliamentary form of government and to ensure presidential independence from the legislative branch. As noted earlier, these same concerns lay behind the Framers' rejection of a procedure by which Congress would have chosen the president.

Disputes over Electors' Appointments

Federal statutory law leaves it to the states—at least in the first instance—to resolve disputes about the validity of a putative elector's appointment (Title 3, section 5, of the U.S. Code—see Appendix B). That federal law provides that state law "shall be conclusive, and shall govern in the counting of electoral votes," if the state law meets three conditions. It must (1) be "enacted prior to the day fixed for the appointment of the electors"—that is, before the date on which the popular election is held in November; (2) provide for the state's "final determination" of any controversy about an elector's appointment; and (3) require that that final determination be made "six days before" the meeting of the electors in the state in mid-December.

First enacted in 1887 (and later reenacted in a codification of laws on presidential selection), this statute represented an effort by Congress to wash its hands of these matters after the disputed Hayes-Tilden election in 1876. The purpose of the statute is to leave to the states disputes over the identity of their electors.

Among other things, the federal law is clear that a state may not, in effect, change the rules after the game is over. The thrust of the federal statute is that if electors are selected under one set of state rules, those rules continue to apply for federal electoral purposes even if the state changes them in midgame.

Federal law does not, however, address several other key questions. For example, how complete must a state's dispute-resolving mechanism be? Does any procedure suffice? Could a state, for example, leave all disputes to the chair of the state Democratic party for resolution? What happens if a state simply does not enact a statute that meets these requirements and a dispute arises over an elector's appointment? What federal procedures control? Constitutionally, what federally mandated procedures *can* control in light of the Constitution's assignment of the manner of electoral appointment to the state legislature? These issues have not yet been adjudicated by the courts—but that day may come.

Disputes over Electors' Discretion

States theoretically fall into two categories with respect to electors' discretion to vote as they choose: those that have "pledged" electors and those that have "unpledged" electors. In twenty-four states, and the District of Columbia, electors are compelled to pledge faithfulness to the presidential candidate with whom they are associated. In some of those states, the compulsion flows directly from state law, as in California, which statutorily requires electors to vote for the candidate of the political party they represent.[12] In other states, the law imposes no such requirement. For example, Minnesota, like many states, leaves it entirely to the political parties to extract pledges from their nominees for elector.[13] If the party fails to do so, the elector is—at least formally—unpledged, having no obligation to vote for any candidate. As discussed later in this chapter in connection with the Bailey case, however, the matter is a bit more complicated: if the voters have a reasonable expectation that an elector will vote for the presidential candidate for whom the voter votes, it might not matter that a political party has been derelict in failing to secure a pledge to that effect. In any event, the number of "unpledged" electors has been significant in only one election, 1960. In that year, fourteen electors from Mississippi and Alabama were elected unpledged and cast their votes for Sen. Harry Byrd (D-Va.). As this experience suggests, even unpledged electors typically run as a slate, fielding candidates for every electoral slot. In contrast, unaffiliated electors run alone, not as part of a slate. The winner-take-all system, however, makes it impossible to run as an unaffiliated elector. In fact, even where the winner-take-all system is not followed (Maine and Nebraska), state law makes no provision for unaffiliated electors.[14]

As for their actual behavior, pledged electors can be divided into two groups. *Faithful electors* are obliged to vote for a certain candidate and vote as promised. Well over 99 percent of all electors have fallen into this category. (Indeed, some have fallen into this category even after their candidates have fallen. In 1872, electors from three states cast their votes faithfully for the candidate to whom they were pledged, Horace Greeley—on the same day he was buried.) *Faithless electors* are obliged to vote for a certain candidate but do not vote as promised. Although this has happened fewer than a dozen times over the course of 200 years— hardly an endemic problem since over 17,000 electors have been chosen since 1789—in the right circumstances a combination of unpledged and faithless electors could change the course of an election.

⌐The Supreme Court addressed the issue of faithless electors most squarely in *Ray v. Blair* (1952)—see Appendix C.¹⁵ In that case, the State of Alabama in effect required candidates for the position of elector to pledge to vote for the nominee of their respective political parties in the electoral college. The supreme court of Alabama concluded that the requirement violated the Twelfth Amendment. It reasoned that the Twelfth Amendment contemplated that electors should be free to vote for the candidate of their choice and that official compulsion to vote for a party's candidate was unconstitutional.

In rejecting this notion on appeal, the U.S. Supreme Court acknowledged that the constitutional text was not controlling. It also found the Framers' intent irrelevant. "As both constitutional provisions long antedated the party primary system," the Court wrote, "it is not to be expected that they or their legislative history would illumine this issue." But the Court found nothing in the Constitution that required a party to accept a candidate for elector who refused to promise to support its presidential and vice-presidential nominees. "Neither the language of Art. II, § 1," the Court said, "nor that of the Twelfth Amendment forbids a party to require from candidates in its primary a pledge of political conformity with the aims of the party." In rejecting the argument that the Twelfth Amendment demands absolute freedom for electors to vote their own choice, uninhibited by a pledge, the Court accorded great weight to political custom:

It is true that the Amendment says the electors shall vote by ballot. But it is also true that the Amendment does not prohibit an elector's announcing his choice beforehand, pledging himself. The suggestion that in the early elections candidates for electors—contemporaries of the Founders—would have hesitated, because of constitutional limitations, to pledge themselves to support party nominees in the event of their selection as electors is impossible to accept. History teaches that the electors were expected to support the party nominees. Experts in the history of government recognize the longstanding practice. Indeed, more than twenty states do not print the names of the candidates for electors on the general election ballot. Instead, in one form or another, they allow a vote for the presidential candidate of the national conventions to be counted as a vote for his party's nominees for the electoral college. This long-continued practical interpretation of the constitutional propriety of an implied or oral pledge of his ballot by a candidate for elector as to his vote in the electoral college weighs heavily in considering the constitutionality of a pledge, such as the one here required, in the primary.

Yet the Court proceeded to distinguish between the enforceability of an elector's pledge and the constitutionality of requiring that pledge. Even if promises of candidates for the electoral college are legally unenforceable, it said, "it would not follow that the requirement of a pledge in the primary is unconstitutional." This suggests that the issue before the Court was the latter—the constitutionality of requiring a pledge—and that the question of a pledge's enforceability was not considered. This is borne out in the Court's statement of its holding:

We conclude that the Twelfth Amendment does not bar a political party from requiring the pledge to support the nominees of the National Convention. Where a state authorizes a party to choose its nominees for elector in a party primary and to fix the qualifications for the candidates, we see no federal constitutional objection to the requirement of this pledge.

It is well and good that a state has the constitutional power to compel potential electors to pledge faithfulness to the candidate with whom they are taken to be affiliated. As noted earlier, twenty-four states and the District of Columbia require such pledges, and they might be gratified to know that their statutes are valid. But one might well wonder about the ultimate usefulness of a pledge that is not legally enforceable. The Court seemed to want it both ways, being unwilling to pound the final nails in the coffin of the electoral college.

This distinction between constitutionality and enforceability is important because five states have enacted statutes penalizing "faithless electors." These penalties range from fines of $1,000 to fourth-degree felonies. If the Court is to be taken literally, its opinion in *Ray v. Blair* (1952) does not go so far as to uphold those statutes. Their validity was not at issue in *Ray* but could well be challenged in a future election, particularly if more states adopt such penalties. No faithless elector has yet been prosecuted for such action.

Disputes over "Vote Throwing"

The question of a pledge's enforceability looms particularly large when a third-party or independent candidate enters the scene. A George Wallace or Ross Perot would have no preexisting party structure to obtain pledges from potential electors, but many states require that the names of candidates for the electoral college appear in nominating petitions. Thus, the presidential candidate would have an opportunity to extract the same sort of commitment upheld as constitutional in *Ray v. Blair.*[16]

If the reasoning of the majority in *Ray* is correct as applied to established parties, it would seem equally correct as applied to upstart parties or independent candidates. "The requirement of a pledge from the candidate participating in primaries to support the nominee is not unusual," the Court said in *Ray*. "Such a provision protects a party from intrusion by those with adverse political principles." Independent and third-party candidates are, constitutionally, no less entitled to protection from intrusion by those with adverse principles.

An independent or third-party candidate desiring to play the role of broker in the electoral college might well wish to go a step further in binding his or her electoral supporters. In addition to requiring each candidate for elector to pledge to vote for the independent presidential candidate, that candidate might wish to compel potential electors to pledge to vote for another candidate whom that candidate might choose to support in the electoral college. George Wallace evidently attempted to extract such a pledge from his electors in 1968. The danger of "faithlessness" in this case resides in the possibility that the elector will disregard the candidate's directive that the elector cast his or her vote for the presidential candidate's second choice.

The wisdom of enforcing these third-party pledges is one of the many issues throughout the electoral process to which Justice Robert Jackson's words apply. He said that "to whose advantage it will prove in the long run I am not foresighted enough to predict" (see *Ray v. Blair* in Appendix C). The question is, whose second choice should receive the elector's vote: the elector's or the presidential candidate's to whom that elector's vote is pledged? The threat of intrigue and cabal would seem to be greater if a third-party pledge were held binding. The presidential candidate is in a more effective position to coordinate "vote throwing" than is an individual elector and, if the validity of the pledge is upheld, would have greater blocs of votes available for that purpose. Indeed, it can be argued that effective, large-scale deal-making is appropriate. No one, after all, is likely to have keener insight into the "principles" to which the electors are pledged than the candidate for whom they promise to vote.

Congressional Challenges to Electors' Votes

On its surface the procedure for congressional objection to an electoral vote is also straightforward. The applicable law is Title 3, section 15, a modern codification of the Electoral Count Act of 1887 (see Appendix B). Section 15 permits Congress to reject those electoral votes not "regularly given." This opportunity for objection occurs on January 6, when members of the House of Representatives and the Senate meet in joint session in the House chamber to count electoral votes. The vice president of the United States presides. The tellers proceed to read and count the electoral votes of the states. After the vote is announced, a member of Congress may rise to object to the counting of a vote from a specified state. After obtaining recognition, the member sends to the desk a written objection setting forth the grounds of the objection.[17] The objection may be signed by additional members of both houses. The Senate then withdraws to its own chamber, and both houses meet separately to consider the objection. Under the statute, debate is strictly limited: no member can speak for more than five minutes (and not more than once), and debate is limited to two hours. At the end of that debate, a vote is taken in each house on whether the objection is agreed to. Both houses must agree to the objection, although each house votes on it even if the other has already rejected it. Only after each house has voted on the objection is the final result announced—even though the disposition of the challenged vote may not affect the election result.[18]

However straightforward it may appear, the process is in reality a constitutional minefield. Inevitably, tension exists between the two constitutional provisions that divide power over electoral proceedings between Congress and state legislatures. The Constitution directs Congress to "count" electoral votes, and it also authorizes each state to select electors "in such Manner as the Legislature thereof may direct."[19] It was under power granted by the first provision that Congress enacted the Electoral Count Act. This statute authorizes Congress, in counting electoral votes, to count only those "regularly given." If an objection is sustained in both houses of Congress to a vote because it is not "regularly given," the vote is not counted. What happens, however, when Congress refuses to count as not "regularly given" a vote that is nonetheless given "in such manner" that a state legislature has prescribed?

In the past, even before enactment of the Electoral Count Act, Congress has declined to count certain electoral votes. For example, after the elections of 1820 and 1832 Congress rejected votes on technical grounds. Votes cast in 1872 were rejected because they had been cast for a deceased candidate (Horace Greeley). And a vote cast in the election of 1880 was rejected because it had been cast on the wrong day.

The Bailey Case. Rather surprisingly, though, no genuine constitutional controversy arose over an elector's failure to vote in accordance with the terms of his or her appointment until the election of 1968. That year, a dispute arose over whether Congress had the power to decline to count the vote of a faithless elector. The objection, entered by Rep. James O'Hara (D-Mich.) and Sen. Edmund Muskie (D-Maine), was made to the vote cast from North Carolina for George Wallace and Curtis Lemay. It was based on the fact that Richard Nixon and Spiro Agnew had won a plurality of votes in that state, that the state's electors were appointed to vote for Nixon and Agnew, and that a vote for Wallace and Lemay was not "regularly given." The one vote cast for Wallace and Lemay was that of Lloyd Bailey, who had announced his intention to do so after his selection as a Nixon-Agnew elector but before the December meeting of the North Carolina electors. Initially, Senate proponents of the objection proposed not simply that the vote cast for Wallace be rejected, but also that it be counted as a vote for Nixon. That proposal was dropped, however, in the concern that the House might not go that far; under the statute, both houses must take the same action if the objection is to be sustained.

Proponents of the objection did not contend that Bailey had not been validly elected. Rather, they argued that the authority to count implies the authority not to count, and that the vote of a faithless elector is not "regularly given" and can therefore not be counted. Bailey, it was said, was a faithless elector. Senator Muskie contended that "the entire process . . . was geared to the assumption that [Bailey] had been nominated by district convention to be a Republican elector, that his nomination as such had been filed without his objection with the appropriate State officials, and that his party's candidate for President had gone on the ballot, carrying his vote with it." [20] And by Bailey's own announcement, he voted for Wallace, not Nixon. Muskie acknowledged that "it is clear that the Constitutional Convention intended that presidential electors shall be free agents"—unless "they, by their act, have previously limited the scope of their freedom." Congress, it was suggested, would simply encourage electoral faithlessness by counting the Bailey vote.

Opponents of the objection argued that the Constitution says simply that the votes should be counted—not that they should be rejected. Congress, they contended, had no right to tell the voters of North Carolina they had one less elector than the number to which they were entitled. Indeed, Congress could not take an ethical obligation and convert it into a constitutional obligation. They maintained that, in the end, the effort represented an attempt to vitiate the role of the electoral college and arrogate to Congress the power to elect the president and vice president since the "faithless elector" phenomenon was inherent in the system as structured. The precedent could permit, for example, a Democratic Congress to disregard electoral votes cast for a Republican presidential candidate and declare the Democratic candidate to have been elected instead.

In the end, both the House and the Senate failed to sustain the objection, thus counting the "faithless" vote of Bailey. But a disturbing amount of confusion permeated the debate on both sides of the issue. Numerous members of both houses debated whether electors were free agents under the Constitution. Few recognized that the Constitution gives the choice to the states. Few focused on action taken—or not taken—by the North Carolina legislature. Had they done so, they might have wondered whether Bailey was in fact a "pledged" elector. Sen. Sam Ervin (D-N.C.) pointed out that more than six days before the meeting of the electors the governor of North Carolina certified as required by federal law that Bailey had been appointed in accordance with the laws of North Carolina. There was, he observed, no set of competing electoral returns from North Carolina. As to the North Carolina law, Senator Muskie acknowledged that "North Carolina makes no provision one way or another with respect to the effect of a North Carolina elector's freedom of choice." [21] Rep. Walter Jones (D) of North Carolina produced a telegram from that state's deputy attorney general stating flatly that "under the North Carolina statutes a presidential elector is not required to cast his vote for any particular candidate." [22] This confirmed a law review article from which Senator Ervin read concluding that "[n]either the old [North Carolina] law, nor the new law ... pledges the elector to cast a party vote, and legally, at least, the individual elector, as was intended by the framers, still has discretion to cast his vote for whomsoever he individually desires." [23] "Consequently," Senator Ervin said, "Dr. Bailey was not bound to vote a party ticket." [24] "His vote was regularly given in the manner prescribed by the Constitution." [25] Testifying in the Senate afterward, Bailey himself said, "There was no discussion of party loyalty, there was no pledge, and there was no commitment made to any candidate." [26]

The Bailey dispute presented two important questions. First, in the event an elector is faithless to his or her pledge, in what department of government does the remedy lie, Congress or the state legislature? Second, what precisely is a "faithless elector"?

There is no reason to believe that, constitutionally, any federal interest should control. Where the state is one in which the electors are expected to choose the nominee of the party they represent, an elector who acts contrary to that expectation has disregarded a duty under that state's law and is subject to that state's legal and equitable remedies to compel a faithful casting of the electoral vote. That a duty flowing from state law has been breached does not imply that Congress, rather than the state, has the constitutional power to remedy that breach. Congress, after the Hayes-Tilden debacle, sought to escape a recurrence by assigning these matters to the states for resolution. This was made clear in the 1886 report of the House Select Committee on the Election of the President and the Vice President on legislation that became the Electoral Count Act. The report explained that the act provided that state courts should determine whether a vote from that state is legal. It also provided that "the two Houses shall be bound by this determination." The committee concluded that "it will be the State's own fault if the matter is left in doubt." [27]

It has been assumed thus far that states' statutes are clear about whether an elector is bound or unbound, and thus whether the vote cast is faithful or faithless. In fact, as suggested above, in some states the matter is left open because state law leaves it to political parties to extract pledges from candidates for elector whom they appoint. Thus, a considerable grey area exists, which is complicated further by the law of equity. As Sen. Frank Church (D-Idaho) pointed out in the Bailey debate, according to the law of equity, a legally enforceable contract will be found to exist where detrimental reliance flows from a promise to perform a certain act. "[S]ince Dr. Bailey represented to the people of North Carolina that he would vote for Mr. Nixon, [and] since they presumably voted for him in order to support the Nixon candidacy, . . . under the doctrine of estoppel he should be bound to that commitment." [28]

The argument is not airtight; the law requires the reasonable expectation that the promisee will demonstrate reliance. Circular as it may be, the general uncertainty surrounding the obligations of electors may itself render any reliance unreasonable. Furthermore, state and federal candidates obviously make campaign promises to the voters and are supported because of their supposed commitments. No one would suggest, however, that those promises are legally enforceable. Still, unlike officeholders, pledged electors are appointed to carry out only one task—to cast a ballot for specified candidates for president and vice president—and there can be no question whether that commitment is honored or breached. These considerations might prove relevant if a future Bailey case were litigated in state courts.

Faithless Electors' Votes. Suppose, in any event, that Bailey had been a "faithless elector." Does Congress have the constitutional power to decline to count his vote for that reason? The better view seems not. As the Bailey precedent demonstrates, "faithful" and "faithless" elector are oversimplified categories. In reality, the measure of discretion exercised by an elector is a function of a blend of statutory provisions and voluntarily assumed commitments that fall somewhere along a spectrum at a point determined by each state legislature. The "problem" of the faithless elector is created largely by a state's legislature, and if that legislature truly considers it a problem, the legislature can fix it.

But a legislature intent on eliminating faithless electors must be careful. Several solutions would not work. The legislature might, for example, permit parties within the state to require pledges of loyalty from candidates for elector—but there is no guarantee that the elector will vote as expected. The legislature might impose criminal or civil penalties on electors who breach that pledge—but a faithless elector might still be willing to pay the price. The legislature might seek an injunction to issue a writ of mandamus to lie in the event an elector announces ahead of time an intention to breach that pledge— but most faithless electors would not be so foolish.

The best solution might be to permit states to enact statutes deeming an elector's vote made in violation of his or her pledge to be null and void. The difficulty, however, is that federal law sets up a procedure that makes this impossible. Electors are required to sign their voting certificates (see Title 3, section 9, in Appendix B), so there is no expectation of secrecy. But from that point on there is no opportunity for any state official to intervene in the process to ensure that the certificate is "faithful," as certificates are then mailed to the vice president of the United States. Congress should permit states to enact the one solution that would work: determining officially that a faithless vote is null and void. It could do so by permitting a state official—say, the secretary of state—to review the certificates and to transmit only those votes cast in accordance with state law. The state has similar authority at an earlier stage in the process, which requires the governor of each state to communicate to the archivist of the United States the names of all valid electors (section 6). The possibility for abuse would not seem measurably greater if the state were empowered to judge the validity of an elector's vote, just as it is empowered to judge the validity of an elector's credentials.

If the task of weeding out "faithless" electoral votes is thus left to the states, what votes fall within the scope of Congress's power not to count because they are not "regularly given"? The meaning of the phrase "regularly given" is not altogether clear. Senator Ervin argued during the Bailey debate that "it means simply that the vote must be given or cast in the manner prescribed by the Constitution." [29] The same statute (Title 3), he noted, also provides that "[t]he electors shall vote for President and Vice President, respectively, in the manner directed by the Constitution." This requires simply that the electors meet on the day fixed by the Constitution and that they vote two ballots (for president and vice president)—as prescribed by the Constitution.

Such a construction of Title 3 would be consistent with the widespread dissatisfaction with congressional involvement in the process following the Hayes-Tilden election. The whole thrust of the reform effort was to expand the role of the states and to reduce, not enhance, the congressional role in judging the validity of electoral votes. Thus, a proposal was defeated that would have permitted the House and Senate, acting jointly, to reject the electoral votes of a state. And the provision that became section 15 of Title 3, pertaining to instances in which more than one set of returns is received from a state, was included (according to the conference committee) to ensure "the counting of lawfully certified votes of states, objections of a Senator or Representative to the contrary notwithstanding." Indeed, the conference committee report said that the purpose of the act was to "circumscribe to a minimum" the power of Congress to disenfranchise a state. [30]

But it would not undercut state authority to read section 15 a bit more expansively. It should be interpreted as permitting Congress to reject not only votes cast in a manner inconsistent with the Constitution but also those cast in a manner that would reasonably be regarded as improper in light of commonly accepted legal principles. Suppose, for example, that evidence is cited that a given electoral vote was cast erroneously, or under duress, or fraudulently, or for an ineligible candidate? Suppose the governor (under section 6) wrongly certified the credentials of an elector who was in fact not chosen? Congress under such circumstances should be seen as authorized not to count these votes because they are not "regularly given."

The congressional objection procedure may never be employed in a situation in which the outcome of the objection would affect the outcome of the election. It has, after all, been in effect for over 100 years without playing a determinitive role in any electoral contest. If the risk is small, though, the stakes are great. Should the day ever come when the smooth operation of the procedure is critical, it may be discovered that it is too elaborate and more likely to generate electoral uncertainty than to remove it.

The rigid debate limitations on congressional objections reflect the drafters' recognition that time is of the essence. Unfortunately, the process set out in the law, if played out in full—including court challenges and appeals, in state and federal courts—could delay a final result until long after January 20.

Dean L. Kinvin Wroth has recommended amending the Electoral Count Act to make federal jurisdiction exclusive over contests concerning presidential electors.[31] This would provide a uniform set of rules and uniform hearing schedule to ensure a timely resolution of electoral disputes and lessen the chance of interfering with the inaugural schedule. An ironclad judicial timetable would surely be an improvement, but one wonders whether any procedure can be thought through so carefully as to eliminate completely the delays for which litigation is infamous. Leaving the validity of an elector's credentials and vote to state authorities would be a big step toward the simple, determinative procedure required. It would not be a complete solution because litigation could arise concerning allegedly "wrongful" gubernatorial action, but a statute could be drafted to compel quick action by the courts and to require that they accord the highest deference to a governor's findings. For example, the statute could prohibit judicial invalidation of the governor's finding only if that finding is arbitrary or capricious or clearly erroneous.

One final potential problem with the congressional objection procedure deserves only cursory attention. It might be suggested that the objection procedure constitutes a form of legislative veto, thus requiring presentation for presidential signature or veto. In *I.N.S. v. Chadha* (1983),[32] the Supreme Court held that Congress legislates when it affects the legal rights of persons beyond the legislative branch. This, arguably, is precisely what Congress does when it deprives an electoral vote of legal force and effect by sustaining an objection. While such an action is technically within the scope of the *Chadha* test, it is doubtful that the Constitution requires that a congressional objection be presented to the president. During the Bailey debate, Sen. Carl Curtis (R-Neb.) pointed out, correctly, that the Senate was not engaged in a lawmaking function:

[T]he Senate is not called upon to perform a legislative duty at this time. We are not here to advance a proposal to become a statute. We are not here called upon to advance an amendment to the Constitution. We have met today to perform a ministerial, quasi-judicial function—the counting of the electoral vote.[33]

The Constitution assigns the task of counting electoral votes to Congress, not—like the function of lawmaking—to Congress and the president. The president thus should have no role in the decision by Congress not to count a given electoral vote. Congressional objection to a vote not regularly given, even though not subject to presidential veto, is not properly regarded as a legislative veto.

Conclusion

 The Constitution is not clear about where final authority rests to regulate the casting of electoral votes. It gives each state the power to choose electors "in such Manner as the Legislature thereof may direct." Yet it also gives Congress the power to count electoral votes. Thus, in a variety of circumstances a state might claim to have determined the "manner" in which an elector was chosen—an elector whose vote Congress refuses to count. Until these issues are resolved by the courts, disputes will continue to arise about where the power of the states ends and the power of Congress begins. All the while, the chances will be enhanced that the electoral college will deadlock, throwing the election into the House of Representatives. How the House selects a president and the Senate a vice president is the subject of the next chapter.

NOTES

1. Smith-Hurd Illinois Annotated Statutes, chapter 46, section 21-1(b).
2. California Election Code, section 25105.
3. *Buckley v. Valeo,* 424 U.S. 1, (1976) at 126.
4. Connecticut General Statutes Annotated, section 9-176.
5. *Powell v. McCormack,* 395 U.S. 486 (1969).
6. Article I, section 5, clause 1.
7. *McPherson v. Blacker,* 146 U.S. (1892) at 27, 35.
8. Connecticut General Statutes Annotated, sections 9-453b through 9-453d, 9-453i.
9. *Williams v. Rhodes,* 393 U.S. 23 (1968) at 24.
10. *McPherson v. Blacker,* 146 U.S. 1 (1892) at 36.
11. *Williams v. Rhodes,* 393 U.S. 23 (1968) at 49, 56, 38, 41-42.
12. California Election Code, section 25105.
13. Minnesota Statutes Annotated, section 208.03, Supp.
14. See Maine Revised Statutes, title 21-A, section 354, Supp.; and Revised Statutes of Nebraska, section 32-504(3).
15. *Ray v. Blair,* 343 U.S. 214 (1952) at 224 n. 11, 225, 228-230.
16. Id. at 221-222, 235.
17. For the text of the most recent objection, see U.S. Congress, House, *Congressional Record,* daily ed., 91st Cong., 1st sess., January 6, 1969, 146.
18. U.S. Congress, Senate, *Congressional Record,* daily ed., 91st Cong., 1st sess., January 6, 1969, 198.
19. Article I, section 1, clause 2.
20. U.S. Congress, Senate, *Congressional Record,* January 6, 1969, 200.
21. Ibid., 212.
22. U.S. Congress, House, *Congressional Record,* January 6, 1969, 164.
23. Ervin, citing 11 N.C. L. Rev. 229 (1932-33) in: U.S. Congress, Senate, *Congressional Record,* January 6, 1969, 202.
24. Ibid., 205.
25. Ibid., 207.
26. U.S. Congress, House, *Congressional Record,* daily ed., 91st Cong., 1st sess., February 5, 1969, 2982.
27. U.S. Congress, House Select Committee on the Election of the President and the Vice President, H.R. Rep. 1638, 49th Cong., 2d sess., 18 *Congressional Record,* 30, (1886).
28. U.S. Congress, Senate, *Congressional Record,* January 6, 1969, 214.
29. Ibid., 207.
30. U.S. Congress, House Select Committee on the Election of the President and the Vice President.
31. L. Kinvin Wroth. "Election Contests and the Electoral Vote," *Dickinson Law Review* 65 (1960-61): 321-353.
32. *I.N.S. v. Chadha,* 462 U.S. 919 (1982).
33. U.S. Congress, Senate, *Congressional Record,* January 6, 1969, 219.

Chapter 4

Roles of the House of Representatives and the Senate in the Electoral Process

Role of the House of Representatives

, It would be "unsafe," Alexander Hamilton wrote in the *Federalist* No. 68, to permit less than a majority of the electoral college to pick a president. Thus, if no candidate receives a majority of the votes cast in the electoral college, the Constitution calls on the House of Representatives to choose the president. Hamilton trusted the House to select "the man who in their opinion may be best qualified for the office." Yet James Madison regarded the House role as so undermining the "Republican principle of numerical equality" and the "federal rule" of numerical equality of the states that a constitutional amendment was "justly called for by all its considerate and best friends." [1] Thomas Jefferson shared Madison's distaste for House participation, which he regarded as "the most dangerous blot on our Constitution." [2] It is not hard to see why. By voting for his or her respective state, the one representative from Vermont (or Montana, Alaska, North Dakota, South Dakota, or Wyoming) casts a vote equal to the votes cast by all fifty-two of California's representatives. Indeed, California's vote may not count at all if no candidate is able to muster a majority.

Parliamentary systems frequently are contrasted with the U.S. system, particularly the manner in which the chief executive is selected. In a parliamentary system, it is pointed out, the prime minister is a member of parliament whose party holds a majority of seats in that body. In the United States, the president is selected not by the legislature but by the electoral college, whose members, today, are selected by the people. Yet as this chapter discloses, the distinction between the two systems is not quite so sharp: the president is sometimes chosen by Congress, and, indeed, the Framers expected that the president would more often be chosen by Congress than by the electoral college. George Mason, in fact, predicted that the House would decide nineteen of twenty presidential elections. But such predictions proved a bit wide of the mark: as discussed earlier, only two elections—those of 1800 and 1824—were decided by the House.

Procedure

The specific steps in the process of selecting a president in this "contingent" House election—contingent upon an electoral college deadlock—are found in both constitutional rules and ad hoc procedures devised in the House of Representatives to meet the remaining questions (see Appendix D).

The Twelfth Amendment (Appendix A) requires that in the event of a deadlock in the electoral college the House "immediately" choose the president "by ballot" from the three presidential candidates receiving the highest numbers of votes in the electoral college. In doing so, "the votes shall be taken by states, the representation from each state having one vote." A quorum, consisting of a member or members from two-thirds of the states, must be present. But a "majority of all the states" is necessary to win.

This bare-bones outline has been fleshed out by precedent in the two "contingent" elections decided by the House (see Chapter 2). A number of issues not addressed in the constitutional text have thus been resolved in parliamentary practice. Rules adopted by the House supersede earlier, nonconstitutional precedents. In the absence of such new rules, however, precedents normally are honored.

A number of significant procedural questions arose in the elections of 1800 and 1824. In one instance—ballot secrecy—the House precedents under which those questions were resolved have constitutional ramifications. In other instances, however, the Constitution does not dictate an answer, and the issues are open to a new approach sensitive to changed times and circumstances. The principal questions surrounding the House selection of a presidency are discussed in the sections that follow.

Decision by the New Congress or Old Congress?   The text of the Constitution does not specify whether the president is to be selected by the "old," lame-duck House of Representatives or the "new" House. Before 1933, the Constitution might have been read to have provided for election by the old House since the new House and the president took office on the same date. Under current statutory law, however, a contingent election would be conducted by the new House.

In 1801 and 1825, selection of the president was thus carried out by the old House of Representatives. But in those years, again, the new Congress was not sworn in until March 4, the same date on which the term of the new president began. In 1933, however, the Twentieth Amendment took effect and specified that the term of the new president begins on January 20 and the term of the new Congress on January 3 (see Appendix A).

Nothing in the Constitution prohibits the old House of Representatives from selecting the president. Federal law currently provides that electoral votes will be counted on January 6, three days after the new Congress is sworn in. To permit the old Congress to choose the president, this statute would therefore have to be changed, placing the electoral vote count on a date before January 3.

One argument for permitting the old House to choose the president is that some of its members—truly "lame" ducks—will not have run for reelection and will not, therefore, have encumbered their votes with pledges to support or oppose a given presidential candidate (supposing that the election should go to the House). Such representatives might be able to exercise a greater degree of independence in casting their votes. In addition, moving up the date would afford more time to conduct the process, which may be why earlier the task was placed in the hands of the old House.

Other observers might argue that the new president should be elected by representatives who have run for office concurrently. To the extent that they have confronted the same issues in their own campaigns, a president elected by new representatives is more likely to reflect the current popular views on those issues rather than the view repudiated recently at the polls. The argument about the time period is valid: thirteen days does not provide enough leeway in the event congressional objections to electoral votes are sustained and challenged in the courts, or in the event the selection process in the House simply bogs down.

But the proper response to the possibility of an election snagged in parliamentary maneuvering and litigation is not to extend the period during which it can occur. The proper response is to eliminate the delay by untangling the procedure—by, for example, federalizing jurisdiction in the event of challenges to electoral votes or giving state governors power to certify the validity of electoral votes (as discussed earlier). The country has much to lose if uncertainty about the identity of the next president drags on for weeks or even months. The election should be conducted by the new House, which will have a greater incentive to wind up matters quickly.

Open or Closed Proceedings?   The Constitution does not indicate whether the House proceedings must be open to the public. In 1801 and 1825, the proceedings were closed. House rules in effect in 1825 limited access to senators, stenographers, and the officers of the House.

In favor of continuing that practice is the traditional confidentiality that has surrounded the making of personnel decisions. Public institutions, such as federal agencies and congressional committees, have opened nearly all meetings to the public—with the exception of meetings on the hiring and firing of agency or committee personnel. Candor is needed in such decisions, and the possibility of candor would be squelched by the presence of reporters and television cameras. Moreover, candid discussion could needlessly damage the reputations of those under consideration.

One could argue, however, that selection of the president of the United States is not simply another "personnel" decision. The decision must, above all, be legitimate in the eyes of the American people. "Next to the propriety of having a President the real choice of a majority of his constituents," Madison wrote, "it is desirable that he should inspire respect and acquiescence by qualifications not suffering too much by comparison." [3] In an era of relentless distrust of government, the selection of a president behind the closed doors of the U.S. House of Representatives could seriously undermine the winner's mandate. This assumes, of course, that secrecy can in fact be achieved. More likely, the process would be marred with rumors and leaks, as it was in 1801 and 1825. Closed-circuit television and live television coverage have become part of the process. It is better that the House not attempt to turn back time: the best antidote to suspicion is openness. The House should stick to its live televised sessions. Although not required constitutionally, the proceedings should be open.

Majority or Plurality of a State's Delegation?   Another issue is what percentage of a state's delegation must vote for a presidential candidate for the state's vote to count. The constitutional text provides merely that in the House "the votes shall be taken by states, the representation from each state having one vote." Nothing is said about whether approval by a majority or plurality of a state's delegates is required to cast the state's vote for a presidential candidate. Consequently, when the issue arises, it must be decided by House rules.

In 1801, the issue did not arise and the rules were silent on this point. Only two candidates competed—Thomas Jefferson and Aaron Burr—and one necessarily would receive a majority. The rules provided simply that if the "ballots of the state be equally divided, then the word 'divided' shall be written" on the ballot. In that event, no vote was counted. The rules did not specify whether a candidate needed a majority rather than a plurality.

But in 1825, with three candidates running in the House, the question was critical. Under new rules a state's vote was to be cast for the candidate "who shall receive a majority of the votes given." Thus, the majority requirement seems to apply to the majority of those actually voting, not to a majority of the entire state delegation in the House. This same requirement is set out in the current rule, which provides that "[i]n all cases of ballot a majority of the votes given shall be necessary to an election" (see Appendix D).

The case for retaining a majority requirement centers on the need for legitimacy in the election results. Public confidence in the outcome is likely to correlate with the margin of the winner; in any election, a candidate who achieves victory with a 35 percent plurality is less likely to be recognized as the winner "as of right" than one who commands, say, a 60 percent majority. For this reason, it might be argued, the Constitution imposes requirements of majority approval in other, similar contexts. A majority of electoral votes is required for victory in the electoral college, and a majority of the states' votes is required for victory in the House. The same rationale ought to apply to votes within state delegations.

All this being said, an election may be too close for any one candidate to command a majority within the House delegation of some states. To decline to count a state's vote because its House delegation is split, say, 10-6-6 would be to disenfranchise that state's voters. In such circumstances, the legitimacy of the election would be undermined rather than enhanced. Furthermore, requiring a majority could prolong the process or even prevent a decision by the House.

In the end, these considerations seem the weightiest and should be deemed controlling, counseling the propriety of permitting states' votes to be decided by pluralities of their delegations. But reasonable arguments can be made on both sides, and it becomes a matter of weighing one set of risks against another. How great is the risk of public nonacceptance of a plurality winner compared with the risk of no winner—with the nation governed, perhaps, for up to four years by an acting president? (As discussed in Chapter 3, if the electoral college deadlocks, the Senate selects a vice president from the two highest on the list.) Would an acting president be accepted by the public? Would the public be less likely to accept an acting president than a president who emerges from election by the House? If no president were picked by the House, would public dissatisfaction be focused more on the House than on the acting president?

These kinds of questions are as numerous as they are unanswerable. The historical track record is simply too short and too distant (consisting, again, only of the elections of 1800 and 1824) to provide enough data for reliable analysis. The answers are likely to be little more than best guesses based on political trends and personalities. In some years, for example, vice-presidential candidates have drawn high praise and would have been generally accepted as president; in other years, their succession to the presidency would have been unthinkable. But the greatest risk, again, would seem to rest in nondecision by the House—a risk that can be reduced by not requiring a majority vote in each delegation.

Secret or Public Ballots?   The Constitution addresses the manner of voting somewhat cryptically. The Twelfth Amendment provides that in the event of electoral college deadlock, the House of Representatives "shall choose immediately, by ballot, the President." This reference to "ballot" is seen by some as the source of a constitutional requirement that votes in the House be secret. The Constitution does not specify whether the "ballot" voting requirement pertains to votes cast by individual representatives or by the states. The issue arises in each context. Unfortunately, there is nothing in the records of the consideration of the Twelfth Amendment in the House or Senate that sheds any light on intent concerning secret or public votes.

As for representatives' ballots, House rules in effect in 1801 provided that the "Representatives of each State shall, in the first instance, ballot among themselves, in order to ascertain the votes of the States." The rule says nothing about secrecy in voting by those representatives. Apparently, votes cast by representatives were secret, although some became public knowledge. On the thirty-sixth ballot, some of Burr's previous supporters cast blank ballots, allowing Jefferson to win. Still, there is no official record of how any representative voted.

The language of the rule in effect in 1825 was virtually identical, and again individual representatives appear to have cast their votes in secret. The official House journal contains no record of any representative's vote. During debate on a proposed amendment to the rule, Daniel Webster referred to the constitutionally protected secrecy of each representative's ballot, and the answer was given that members' "privilege of a secret ballot" within their state delegation was secure. In subsequent House debates, it has been believed that the Twelfth Amendment "by ballot" requirement entails a written secret vote within the state delegations.

If the House was correct in its apparent belief that the Twelfth Amendment required secret representative ballots, that interpretation cannot be overturned by rule or ruling; the Constitution prevails over any contrary statute, parliamentary order, or ruling of the chair. Yet the House, in revisiting these procedures, might simply conclude that its earlier construction of the phrase "by ballot" was incorrect, or that the meaning of "by ballot" has in effect changed over the decades as governmental processes have become more open.

What are the institutional consequences of secret versus public representatives' ballots? On the one hand, it should, arguably, be difficult for a representative to break a campaign pledge to support a certain candidate if the election goes to the House. There is, of course, no requirement that a representative undertake any such pledge. If he or she does so, however, democratic principles might suggest the propriety of making it harder rather than easier for the representative to evade the pledge. This consideration militates in favor of a recorded vote.

On the other hand, secret ballots would make it easier to change votes on subsequent ballots and would make bargaining more difficult, thus minimizing the possibility of a deadlock in the House. For this reason, the case for secret ballots is stronger if the rules provide for decision by a majority rather than a plurality of each state delegation. If three strong candidates were to run, public ballots combined with a majority vote requirement would raise a serious possibility of deadlock.

Delegations' ballots, however, are another story. Although the Twelfth Amendment was adopted after the election of 1800, the original language of Article II on the use of ballots in the House of Representatives was virtually identical (see Appendix A).

In 1801, as in 1825, the ballots cast by states were secret. In neither case is there any notation in the official journal of proceedings as to how any state cast its vote. The journal records only the number of states that voted for each candidate on each ballot. Several newspapers, however, did report how both states and delegates voted in both 1801 and 1825.

Still, there seems little constitutional reason to believe that secret ballots are required on the state level. Even if the Constitution requires secret representative ballots, it is not persuasive to argue (as did Daniel Webster) that state ballot secrecy is necessary to protect representative ballot secrecy. Today, as a matter of political reality, it is not practical to think that the vote of a state delegation can be kept secret.

• *What Quorum Is Required?*   Like the issue of ballot secrecy, the question of what quorum is necessary for voting arises at two levels: within the state delegations and within the House itself.

The Constitution is altogether silent on the quorum requirement—if any—applicable to voting within state delegations. As indicated earlier, the rules applicable in 1801 did not address the issue, and those applicable in 1825 required that the winner have a "majority of votes given," implying the absence of any quorum requirement. The current rules, again, also refer to "votes given" (see Appendix D).

The issue of what quorum is required may seem technical, but it is not hard to envision circumstances in which the quorum requirement becomes critical. With no quorum requirement, if only one member happens to be present, that member can bind the entire delegation. A quorum requirement of two-thirds, however, presents possibilities for mischief. Assume, for example, that three candidates have roughly equal strength within a given state delegation. Assume that some of the supporters of one of the candidates defect and combine forces with the delegates of one of the remaining candidates. And assume that that candidate then commands just over a majority of that state's delegation. If the rule requires merely that the winner have a "majority of votes given," that candidate wins the state's vote. But if the rule sets out a quorum requirement equal to that for the House itself—two-thirds—then when the opponents of a candidate number more than one-third but lack a majority, it makes sense for the opponents to walk out, thus denying a quorum and barring the state from voting. In this way, a minority can prevent the majority of the delegation from casting the state's vote for the candidate the majority prefers.

On the matter of a quorum for the entire House, the Twelfth Amendment is explicit: a "member or members from two-thirds of the states" constitutes a quorum. The same requirement was set forth in the original Constitution. Consequently, in both the election of 1800 and the election of 1824 a two-thirds quorum was required.

How Long Is "Immediately"? Finally, the Constitution requires that the House "immediately" choose a president. Yet nothing in the Constitution limits the amount of time or number of ballots the House may devote to selecting a president. The rules of the House reiterated this requirement for both previous House elections. Yet in 1801, Jefferson was not selected until the thirty-sixth ballot, after a week of voting. In 1825, however, only a single ballot was required.

During both previous elections, House rules prohibited the interruption of balloting by other business. This rule should be retained. No other calendar item has or should have the priority of selecting a president. Recess should be permitted during the selection process, however; negotiation is an integral part of the legislative process, and nothing is to be gained if the decision is made by exhausted representatives who have been meeting round-the-clock.

Adoption of Rules Governing Presidential Elections

The rules currently in effect were adopted by the House in 1825 to govern disposition of the election of 1824 (see Appendix D). No substantive revision has occurred since that time. If the House were of the view that the rules need revision because of the kinds of matters just discussed, the question will arise: when should the revised rules be adopted?

In part because two-thirds of the members of the Senate are not up for reelection every two years when Congress adjourns, the Senate considers itself a "continuing body." As such, it has a

continuing set of standing rules; they are not readopted at the beginning of each session.

In contrast, all members of the House face reelection every two years. The House thus does not consider itself a continuing body and proceeds, at the outset of each new Congress, to elect new leaders and to adopt new rules. Of course, the leaders and rules are no different than those of the last Congress, but in principle they can be changed.

All this bears directly on the timing of rule revision and adoption and suggests a parliamentary dilemma in the event the House waits to modernize its rules until it is actually confronted with a contingent presidential election. If the House adopts new rules after the popular vote has indicated the probability of electoral college deadlock, it likely will be accused of trying to tilt the results. Yet House members during one Congress cannot adopt rules that bind House members during the next Congress. Consequently, however evenhanded the effort of the "old" House to draft a neutral set of rules, the "new" House inevitably would be confronted with an effort by dissatisfied blocs to reopen the debate at a moment when time is of the essence— two weeks before the president is scheduled to be inaugurated, and possibly in the midst of congressional objections to electoral votes and derivative litigation.

When faced with these potential complications during the summer of 1992, the House began a review of the House rules on election of the president to examine whether the House should adopt, before the November election, a set of neutral principles that might lay the groundwork for the formal adoption of revised rules by the new Congress. In July, before the process moved much further, independent candidate Ross Perot withdrew from the presidential race, removing any sense of urgency about revision of the rules and letting the House off the hook. Even Perot's later reentry into the race did not prompt the House to act since he was thought unlikely to carry any states.

Rather than waiting until it is again faced with this problem, the House should revise and modernize its rules governing presidential election. Only when a deadlocked electoral college does not loom on the horizon can the House avoid charges of drafting its rules to favor one candidate or another. The time is ripe to draw up modern, neutral rules based on contemporary values of open procedure and fairness to all candidates, regardless of party affiliation or non-affiliation.

Conclusion

⁄ Of the various procedural questions examined above, three are addressed by the Constitution—House quorum size, ballot secrecy, and, arguably, whether a majority or plurality of a state's delegates is necessary to cast its vote. The other questions are left open by the Constitution and can be addressed by the House as it sees fit, based on policy considerations.

Reasonable arguments can be made on both sides of these issues. The one conclusion that does emerge, however, is that like other elements of the presidential selection process, these questions of House procedure have received little public or even congressional attention in modern times. In one sense, that inattention is understandable: these issues have not arisen for 170 years. They may not arise for another 170 years. If they do arise, however, the situation could be politically explosive. There is no need to compound political explosiveness with legal uncertainty. Sooner rather than later, the House should engage in a serious, purposeful review of its presidential selection rules with an eye to thinking through each of the various scenarios that might arise and devising the best possible parliamentary response to each.

Role of the Senate

The Twelfth Amendment provides that if no candidate for vice president has a majority of votes cast in the electoral college, "then from the two highest on the list, the Senate shall choose the Vice President." The Senate has chosen a vice president only once, in · 1837. Martin Van Buren's vice-presidential candidate, Richard M. Johnson, failed by one vote to receive a majority of votes cast for vice president in the electoral college. This occurred even though Martin Van Buren himself did receive a majority of votes cast in the electoral college for president. The reasons for the electoral college's rejection of Johnson apparently were related to disapproval of his social conduct.

No Senate action was necessary in 1801 because, before adoption of the Twelfth Amendment, the candidate finishing second in the House of Representatives automatically became vice president. That candidate was Aaron Burr. In 1825, although no presidential candidate had a majority in the electoral college, a vice-presidential candidate did, John C. Calhoun.

The standing rules of the Senate contain no procedure to be followed in selecting a vice president. In 1837, the Senate adopted a resolution establishing the procedure to be followed. It provided simply that senators would vote by voice (there being no "ballot" requirement of the sort applicable to the House). This was done alphabetically by member rather than by state (as is done in the House). Johnson won 33-16 on a straight party-line vote.

Like its provisions concerning selection of the president by the House, the Twelfth Amendment similarly prescribes a quorum requirement for selection of the vice president by the Senate. It provides that "a quorum for the purpose shall consist of two-thirds of the whole number of Senators, and a majority of the whole number shall be necessary to a choice."

The possibility of abuse of the quorum requirement just described in connection with voting within a state delegation in the House assumes a different form in the Senate. Unlike the House, the two-thirds quorum requirement in the Senate applies to individuals, not states. Although a candidate in principle needs only a simple majority to be selected vice president, in practical reality that candidate needs two-thirds—if every senator opposing that candidate is willing to walk out and deny a quorum. In contrast, in the House it is far more difficult for likeminded members to band together to deny a quorum. If over one-third of House members walked out, it is unlikely that they would be spread over the requisite number of states. In the House, two-thirds of the states—not members— constitute a quorum, and only one member need be present within each delegation to record its presence for quorum purposes.

•The most serious danger is not abuse of the quorum requirement, however. It is the possibility that the vice president chosen by the Senate will have run on a ticket that opposed the president, if a president is indeed selected by the House. And it can be worse than that: it is possible that the Senate might have *no choice* but to select a vice president other than the running mate of the president. The House selects the president from the top three candidates in the electoral college. The Senate, however, selects the vice president from only the top two candidates in the electoral college. Consequently, if the House selects as president the candidate who finished third in the electoral college, and if that candidate's vice-presidential choice also finished third, the Senate is constitutionally precluded from selecting the president's running mate as vice president.

This has never happened. If it appeared likely, it might well be expected to weigh against the Senate's choice of that individual. The problem, however, is that the Senate might not be aware of whom the House has elected president. Indeed, the House might be deadlocked. Under those circumstances, the Senate might well conclude that its task is to move forward rather than delay since the person it chooses as vice president will become acting president.

The policy considerations underlying several issues that arise in the House are basically the same for the Senate. There is no constitutional provision, for example, specifying whether the proceedings should be open or closed. The reasons that support open House sessions also suggest the propriety of open Senate sessions.

Some of the issues that confront the House are not pertinent to the Senate. Because senators vote for vice president individually rather than by state, majority/plurality questions do not arise. Nor is there any requirement that the Senate choose a vice president "by ballot." Thus, constitutionally, the issue of voting secrecy does not arise. The Senate could still act by secret ballot, but the text of the Constitution presents no reason for thinking that that might be required. In addition, all of the policy considerations counseling procedural openness discussed in connection with the House suggest the desirability of a recorded vote in the Senate.

For one final question, however, the Senate is on a different constitutional footing than the House. That is the issue of whether the old or new House and Senate should choose a president and vice president. As indicated earlier in this chapter, the Constitution does not preclude selection of the president by the old House, although the statutory timetable now in effect renders that impossible. That same timetable makes selection of a vice president by the old Senate impossible. The case for changing it to permit selection by the old Senate is slightly different than the case for permitting selection by the old House. The Senate is a continuing body and two-thirds of the membership of the new Senate will necessarily be the same as that of the old Senate, whereas the House, at least in principle, could turn over completely. Still, neither the president nor the vice president should be voted on by a Senate or House composed of members rejected by the voters. In a close vote, that is a formula for instant illegitimacy. It is better that the identity of both president and vice president reflect voter attitudes revealed in the most recent elections.

NOTES

1. Lucius Wilmerding, Jr., *The Electoral College* (New Brunswick, N.J.: Rutgers University Press, 1958), 185.
2. Letter to George Hay (August 17, 1823) reprinted in Paul L. Ford, ed., *The Works of Thomas Jefferson*, Vol. XII (London: G.P. Putnam's Sons, 1905), 303.
3. Wilmerding, *Electoral College*, 192.

Chapter 5

Role of the Courts
in the Electoral Process

Whether and when the courts will intervene is at bottom a policy-oriented inquiry. The recurring question is whether it makes sense for a court to decide *this* dispute, between *these* parties, at *this* time. The legal technicalities may seem complex, but the results typically flow from basic policy considerations about the courts' institutional capacities, the nature of the issue, the character of the parties, and the timing of the litigation.

As one looks over the presidential election procedure, it is obvious that disputes might arise at a number of different points. Eight examples follow.

1. A candidate for elector might challenge a state statute that renders him ineligible to run.

2. A state official or elector might challenge the power of Congress to set a date for the electors' meeting.

3. A voter might challenge the procedure a state has enacted for the selection of electors.

4. A voter or elector might challenge the "conclusiveness" of a state law providing for the appointment of electors or the counting of that state's electoral votes.

5. A voter might challenge a faithless elector's breach of promise or violation of a state law requiring faithfulness, thus raising directly the issue of a pledge's enforceability.

6. An elector might challenge the validity of a candidate's directive throwing that candidate's electoral college votes (including that elector's vote) to another candidate.

7. A candidate, elector, or member of Congress might challenge congressional action sustaining an objection to an elector's vote (as

could have occurred, for example, in the Bailey case).

8. A member of the House of Representatives might challenge a rule of the House governing election of the president—a rule that, say, made public her ballot.

In deciding whether to adjudicate these sorts of issues, the courts confront three basic questions. First, is the issue one that the courts properly can decide? Second, are the proper parties before the court? Third, is the time of litigation appropriate—that is, was the action brought too soon or too late?

It is easy to see, in light of these considerations, that no general answer presents itself for any of the eight hypothetical legal actions. The issue of whether a state statute governing the disposition of electoral disputes is "conclusive" under federal law obviously presents a task more analytically discreet and less politically sensitive than, say, determining the constitutionality of a House rule making electoral ballots public. Similarly, it would be one thing for the courts to entertain a claim of a representative about the validity of such a House rule, but quite another to allow such a claim by a private citizen who can assert no direct injury. And common sense suggests limiting judicial resources to the disposition of "live" disputes, so that a challenge to the enforceability of a faithless elector's promise might well be viewed differently if it has already been broken rather than if it might under some conceivable circumstances be broken. The central question, therefore, of whether a given legal action is appropriate for judicial review is heavily fact-dependent and can be answered only on a case-by-case basis.

In moving from one case to another, the courts have developed three doctrines: political question doctrine, which deals with the "what" question; the doctrine of standing, which deals with the "who" question; and the doctrine of ripeness, which deals with the "when" question.

Political Question Doctrine

Courts rely on the political question doctrine to determine whether an issue is one that can properly be decided by a court. *Baker v. Carr* (1962)[1] set forth the contemporary standard for determining whether the nature of an issue renders it fit for judicial resolution. It specified six different factors that should cause the courts to dismiss a case because it presents a "political question." The first consideration is whether the issue is a "textually demonstrable constitutional commitment of the issue to a coordinate political department." The courts would not, for example, engage in an actual counting of electoral votes because that task is textually committed to the Congress. Another factor that the courts consider is whether the judiciary lacks "discoverable and manageable standards for resolving it." The Supreme Court has, for example, regarded that portion of the Constitution guaranteeing to the states a "Republican Form of Government" ² as presenting a lack of judicially discoverable standards. The third consideration is whether it is possible to decide the issue without making a "policy determination of a kind clearly for nonjudicial discretion." Under this factor, courts can refrain from resolving intensely controversial issues and thereby risking their legitimacy. The fourth consideration is whether the court can resolve the issue without "expressing lack of the respect due coordinate branches of government." The president or Congress (or a state, for that matter) might invest a good measure of political capital in a certain initiative, counseling against its judicial undoing. A fifth consideration is whether there exists "an unusual need for unquestioning adherence to a political decision already made." Sometimes it is more important that a decision be made than that it be made correctly; this may apply to undoing the results of a close presidential election. Finally, the court considers the "potentiality of embarrassment from multifarious pronouncements by various departments on one question." Embarrassment to the president or Congress may result if an act of either is invalidated; the consequences, particularly negative international implications, can lead to judicial abstention.

These tests, taken together, may seem to cover the waterfront, but the Supreme Court has emphasized that *political question* is a term of art. "The doctrine of which we treat," it said in *Baker*, "is one of 'political questions,' not one of 'political cases.' The courts cannot reject as "no law suit" a bona fide controversy as to whether some action denominated 'political' exceeds constitutional authority."

Although this standard is more elaborate than that employed in the nineteenth century, the Court is not inclined to depart from earlier decisions concerning an issue's justiciability. In *McPherson v. Blacker* (1892), it confronted directly the question of whether the Court was capable of resolving the validity of a state's electoral scheme. The Supreme Court gave short shrift to the argument that the political question doctrine precluded it from deciding the case. The argument for resorting to the political question doctrine and dismissing the case was, admittedly, overly broad. In rejecting the contention that "all questions connected with the election of a presidential elector are political in their nature," the Court said:

[T]he judicial power of the United States extends to all cases in law or equity arising under the Constitution and laws of the United States, and this is a case so arising, since the validity of the state law was drawn in question as repugnant to such constitution and laws, and its validity was sustained.[3]

The issue received the same summary treatment in *Williams v. Rhodes* (1968):

Ohio's claim that the political-question doctrine precludes judicial consideration of these cases requires very little discussion. That claim has been rejected in cases of this kind numerous times. It was rejected by the Court unanimously in 1892 in the case of McPherson v. Blacker, ... and more recently it has been squarely rejected in Baker v. Carr (1962), and in Wesberry v. Sanders (1964). Other cases to the same effect need not now be cited. These cases do raise a justiciable controversy under the Constitution and cannot be relegated to the political arena.[4]

Given these firm holdings, it is improbable that the Court will dismiss most actions about the validity of a given federal or state presidential election procedure on the grounds of the political question doctrine.

Doctrine of Standing

The law of standing was summarized by the Supreme Court in *Valley Forge Christian College v. Americans United for Separation of Church and State*.[5] Article III of the Constitution, the Court said, limits the judicial power of federal courts to cases and controversies. This means that a plaintiff must "show that he personally has suffered some actual or threatened injury as a result of the putatively illegal conduct of the defendant" and that the injury "fairly can be traced to the challenged action" and "is likely to be redressed by a favorable decision." To go beyond cases involving real injury to real plaintiffs, the Court said, would be to transgress the notion of separation of powers.

To meet the Court's standing requirement in any one of the eight hypothetical controversies outlined above, it would be necessary for a plaintiff to show personal injury-in-fact that is traceable to the challenged action and will be redressed if the Court grants the challenged relief. For example, in situation (8) a member of the House of Representatives might well be found to have suffered injury-in-fact if a rule of the House unconstitutionally made public his ballot (in an election decided by the House). A member, the argument would go, has a constitutional entitlement to a secret ballot, and that entitlement was breached to his detriment. The result would likely be different, however, if the complaintant were a private citizen. In that case, the citizen would almost surely be found to have suffered no injury-in-fact since the putative entitlement to a secret ballot is that of a member of Congress, not a citizen.

The standing issue has not been litigated authoritatively in the context of presidential election procedure. Accordingly, it is impossible to predict how the Court might come out on this issue; the facts on injury, causation, and remediability vary greatly from one case to the next. It might nonetheless be noted that in recent years the Court has rigidly insisted that plaintiffs meet these requirements.

Doctrine of Ripeness

The doctrine of ripeness addresses *when* a conflict can be decided by a court. A federal district court, confronting the issue of ripeness in 1990 in connection with the Gulf War, said:

It has long been held that, as a matter of the deference that is due to the other branches of government, the Judiciary will undertake to render decisions that compel action by the President or the Congress only if the dispute before the Court is truly ripe, in that all the factors necessary for a decision are present then and there.[6]

Although ripeness requirements are particularly hard to summarize in greater detail, a few Supreme Court cases do provide some illumination. In *UPW v. Mitchell* (1947),[7] the Court noted simply that "a hypothetical threat is not enough." How hypothetical is too hypothetical? The Court used a balancing test in resolving this issue in *Abbott Laboratories v. Gardner* (1967).[8] The principal prudential factors that underlie the determination of ripeness come down to a kind of cost/benefit analysis, so that if an action (such as one of the eight just listed) were to be brought, the courts might ask: What is gained, and what is lost, by waiting?

One rationale often put forward for delay is that the controversy will become more concrete and focused, making it easier to evaluate the practical merits of the parties' positions. Delay in some cases can indeed help clarify issues. But as one commentator has pointed out, that concern has more bearing on cases when the constitutional questions are "extremely close." [9] In other cases, the issues presented are "purely legal, and will not be clarified by further factual development." [10]

A case such as number (5) above, concerning a challenge to a faithless elector's breach of promise or violation of a state law requiring faithfulness, would seemingly fall into the latter category of cases. There the issues would be predominantly legal, in that waiting for the unfolding of further facts "would not . . . significantly advance [the Court's] ability to deal with the legal issues presented nor aid [it] in their resolution." [11]

Another key inquiry in ripeness jurisprudence is the extent to which a delay in judgment will cause hardship.[12] Here, it is not overstating matters to say that a delay in adjudication under certain circumstances could be disastrous. Hypothetical number (1), for example, concerns a candidate for elector challenging a state statute that renders him ineligible to run. Delay until after the injury occurs would result in an election ballot without the candidate's name on it. This consequence would effectively preclude the candidate from running for the office of elector, a hardship that can be avoided only by deciding the case before the injury occurs.

Conclusion

Predicting how judges will decide a case is perilous business, especially in cases with high political stakes. The law is not a big computer in the sky into which facts are fed; indeed, doctrines pertaining to political questions, standing, and ripeness are not applied mechanically by apolitical automatons. Judges, like everyone else, have likes and dislikes, opinions and philosophies, experiences and backgrounds. Their rulings—the law—reflect these predilections, however much they may strive for "objectivity." Try as they might, judges usually remember what president appointed them. They often were active in that president's political party.

Thus, no one should be deluded into thinking that the kinds of controversies hypothesized at the outset of this chapter are resolved solely by reference to legal doctrine. They are not. Nor should anyone believe that legal doctrine is sufficiently determinate to permit reliable prediction in these kinds of cases. It is not. The life of the law, Oliver Wendell Holmes said, is not logic but experience. The nation's experience with these controversies is limited. The law's ability to render predictable answers is no less limited.

NOTES

1. *Baker v. Carr,* 369 U.S. 186 (1962) at 217.
2. Article IV, section 4.
3. *McPherson v. Blacker,* 146 U.S. 1 (1892) at 23.
4. *Williams v. Rhodes,* 393 U.S. 23 (1968) at 28.
5. *Valley Forge Christian College v. Americans United for Separation of Church and State,* 454 U.S. 464 (1982) at 471-72.
6. *Dellums v. Bush,* 752 F. Supp. 1141 (1990) at 1149.
7. *UPW v. Mitchell,* 330 U.S. 75 (1947) at 90.
8. *Abbott Laboratories v. Gardner,* 387 U.S. 136 (1967).
9. Scharph, *"Judicial Review and the Political Question: A Functional Analysis,"* Yale Law Journal 75 (1966): 517, 531-532.
10. *Pacific Gas & Electric Co. v. State Energy Resources Conservation and Development Commission,* 461 U.S. 190, (1983) at 201.
11. Ibid.
12. *Abbott Laboratories v. Gardner,* 387 U.S. 136 (1967) at 149.

Chapter 6

The Legitimacy of the
Electoral Process in the
Eyes of the American Public

A nd now finally back to the question posed in Chapter 1 of this book: Does the original rationale for the electoral college continue to apply? Whatever the merits of retaining deliberative institutions in a republic, clearly the electoral college cannot exercise the role originally contemplated by the Framers. In an era of party slates—following 200 years of evolution of political parties—the electoral college cannot be composed of unpledged electors, all of them free to exercise full discretion in examining issues and all of them independent in selecting a candidate for president. It cannot uproot political parties from the civic soil; it cannot exclude electors who have run and been elected on promises to vote for a specified major-party candidate. The clock cannot be turned back.

The expectations of the American people have evolved over these 200 years. They have, for the most part, come to equate their votes for a president with direct votes for the individual running for president. They have, over 200 years, come to expect their country to be more a democracy than a republic. The legitimacy of the electoral process would shatter if the American electorate were suddenly confronted with a fully revitalized electoral college. James S. Fishkin, distancing himself from the suggestion that the electoral college should now be revived as a deliberative body, put it well: "[M]illions of Americans vote in the expectation that the results will be determined by popular totals. . . . Given these . . . expectations, departures from the vote totals by individual electors rightly produce moral outrage."[1]

In light of these evolved expectations, what role can the public rightly look to the electoral college to play in a nation moving steadily toward greater and greater citizen participation? Is the

electoral college of the Framers the last remaining institutional
dinosaur of a bygone republican age, or is it adaptable to the era of
participatory democracy? Specifically, is every citizen constitutionally entitled to seek the office of presidential elector? Can a
politically unaffiliated candidate—an unpledged candidate who is
not part of any slate—run for elector?

Over the course of American history, only a handful of unaffili-
ated candidates have won election to the office of presidential elector.
In a number of instances, however, electors of two or three parties
have won in the same state. Electors of more than one party won in
New Jersey in 1860; in California in 1880; in North Dakota,
Oregon, and Ohio in 1892; in California and Kentucky in 1896; in
Maryland in 1904 and 1908; in California in 1912; and in West
Virginia in 1916. These electoral "splits" occurred because the states
in question eschewed a pure winner-take-all system and effectively
permitted voters to vote for individual electors.

In *Williams v. Rhodes* (1968),[2] the Supreme Court invalidated
Ohio statutes that made it virtually impossible for a new political
party to be placed on the state ballot to choose presidential electors.
Following *Williams,* suits brought by independent presidential
candidates Eugene McCarthy and John Anderson succeeded in
numerous states in invalidating statutes that were argued to dis-
criminate against such candidates.[3] McCarthy won in Delaware,[4]
Florida,[5] Idaho,[6] Illinois,[7] Kansas,[8] Michigan,[9] Missouri,[10] Nebraska,[11]
New Mexico,[12] Oklahoma,[13] Texas,[14] and Utah.[15] Anderson won in
Florida,[16] Kentucky,[17] Maine,[18] Maryland,[19] New Mexico,[20] North
Carolina,[21] and Ohio.[22]

The *Williams* Court, like the lower courts that followed it, did not
directly address whether a state constitutionally can preclude an
unaffiliated candidate from running for elector. The Court's rationale for striking down the Ohio laws, however, would seemingly
apply to a statute that excludes unaffiliated candidates for elector.
The flaw in the Ohio statutes was that they burdened "the right of
individuals to associate for the advancement of political belief, and
the right of qualified voters, regardless of their political persuasion,
to cast their votes effectively."[23] A statute that excludes unaffiliated
candidates for elector would seemingly burden these same rights.

Yet every one of the forty-eight general-ticket, winner-take-all
states effectively precludes unaffiliated candidates from running for
elector. Each such state, by giving all its electoral votes to the

presidential candidate who receives the greatest popular vote, excludes unaffiliated candidates. Since *Williams,* independent candidates can run for the office of elector if they affiliate with a slate that runs candidates for every electoral slot. But an unaffiliated candidate, interested in winning simply one slot, cannot run in these states. Does this mean that the winner-take-all system in effect in most states for most of this nation's history is unconstitutional?

Not likely. Even though associational and voting rights are burdened by the winner-take-all system, given the enduring prominence of that system it is hard to imagine that an unaffiliated electoral candidate could challenge it successfully. More likely, the Supreme Court would hold that that candidate has a right to compete for the office of elector as part of a slate that runs candidates for every electoral opening. The implication seems to be that there is no right not to associate since a state may, in exercising its plenary authority to determine the manner in which electors are selected, require every candidate for elector to be part of a slate.

Still, states can *permit* unaffiliated candidates to run for the office of elector; they are not (apparently) *required* to do so. As a matter of policy rather than constitutional law, is it a good idea to permit unaffiliated candidates to run for elector? To permit candidates to run for elector without pledging to vote for any presidential candidate would open the presidential selection process to public participation in a variety of ways. "Citizen" candidates might run for elector solely on their position on one or more issues. They might pledge to support whatever candidate for president takes a position closest to their own. They might, for that matter, avoid issues altogether and run on the basis of their background, credentials, or accomplishments, promising merely to exercise their best judgment in voting for a presidential candidate. That presidential candidate may be one of the major parties' nominees, or may be a person who is not a presidential candidate. Of course, the elector's vote might easily be thrown away—but that is one of the issues of judgment and discretion to be weighed during a campaign for appointment as elector.

Such procedural possibilities could provide an electoral "safety valve" for the disaffected. Voters dissatisfied with the choices confronting them on the November ballot would be able to vote, in effect, for "none of the above"—for a third choice, for candidates for elector who agree with their positions on an issue or issues. They could participate in the electoral process without having to vote for the "lesser of two evils." They need not increase the mandate of a candidate they find disagreeable or lend legitimacy to electoral results they find unfortunate. Meeting together, unaffiliated electors could structure deliberative, information-gathering meetings with presidential candidates. Presidential candidates may ignore them if they expect a landslide, but in close elections, with enough independent electors meeting throughout the nation, that course could be perilous.

The danger in partially resurrecting the electoral college lies in the further disaggregation of power promoted by the appointment of unaffiliated electors. The bargaining power of minorities and special interests would be vastly enhanced. If an interest group such as farmers captures, say, twenty electoral votes, and if the margin of difference between the two major-party candidates is fewer than twenty votes, each candidate might be expected to capitulate to agricultural demands—regardless of the national interest—in clamoring for those votes. The resulting problems could approach those of the Israeli parliament, in which a zealous religious minority provided the swing votes necessary to form a government when neither of the main parties could command a parliamentary majority.

The "Dixiecrat" movement illustrated this phenomenon. In 1948, Gov. Strom Thurmond of South Carolina, with 2.4 percent of the popular vote, won thirty-nine electoral votes. Had 12,487 votes shifted in California and Ohio, neither Truman (who won 49.6 percent of the popular vote) nor Dewey (who won 45.1 percent) would have had an electoral college majority—which the addition of those thirty-nine votes would have provided. In 1960, fourteen "unpledged" electors voted for Harry Byrd. Had 8,971 Illinois voters voted for Nixon rather than Kennedy, neither would have had an electoral college majority, and Byrd's fourteen electors would have dictated the outcome.

But this is not an argument merely against the electoral college. It is an argument against any nonproportional, winner-take-all electoral system (which includes both majority-rule systems and plurality-rule systems). In a proportional system, a minority by definition commands only an amount of votes equal to its polling power. But in a winner-take-all system, where a majority or plurality is necessary for victory, and where a minority can provide the marginal votes necessary for victory, that minority receives attention disproportionate to its numbers. Something like this could have occurred in 1968. It was reported that, before the popular election at a time when an electoral college majority for any candidate appeared doubtful, representatives of Richard Nixon met with those of George Wallace in search of votes. Had the election been closer, Wallace's supporters could have been in the catbird seat, as were Israel's right-wing parties for some years.

Nonproportional Representation

In the broadest sense, the presidential election procedure in the United States is at every level nonproportional. The winner-take-all system in effect in all states but Maine and Nebraska is a striking example. The 49 percent of the voters who vote for a loser get nothing; if an additional 1 or 2 percent can be cobbled together with one minority or another, that minority gets what it wants. It is sometimes argued that the district systems of Maine and Nebraska eliminate this problem, but they too are nonproportional: the game is simply shifted from the state level to the district level, where the winner still takes all (the whole district). The same applies to election in the electoral college, where a majority is required; to election in the House of Representatives, where a majority is also required; and to the vote cast within each state delegation in the House, whether a majority or plurality rule is adopted. The phenomenon is inherent in winner-take-all systems.

There are, of course, different arguments at every level for going with a nonproportional, winner-take-all approach. In selecting electors, the nonproportional approach partially negates the tendency of the political system to shortchange discreet and insular ethnic and religious minorities. At the electoral college level, the approach tends to magnify the results of a popular victory. In 1912, for example, Woodrow Wilson received only a 41 percent plurality of the popular vote—but won 81 percent of the electoral votes. It thus lends legitimacy to election results. And it strengthens existing political parties and penalizes newcomers with short-term staying power by effectively disenfranchising all that are unable to command a majority at birth.

But these benefits, again, are not cost-free. Beyond exaggerating the power of special interests, nonproportional systems further distort results. Wilson was not really as popular as the electoral vote suggested; whatever legitimacy the electoral college conferred in 1912 was easily seen through as artificial. A winner-take-all system not only exaggerates results but makes possible wrong results: it is possible for a popular vote winner to lose because of the way the vote is concentrated. (This happened in the elections of 1824, 1876, and 1888.) The system safeguards the two-party system at the cost of stifling political innovation, opting for stability over change. And in doing so it effectively disenfranchises the already disaffected (such as antiwar activists in 1968 and 1972).

Is this what Americans want? Maybe or maybe not, but the point is that they need to keep their eyes on the ball: the real issue is a form of proportional representation versus a winner-take-all system; the electoral college and the contingent House election are merely a manifestation of one form of the latter. And the question is: what is the alternative to the existing multitiered, winner-take-all approach in the presidential selection system?

Proportional Representation

One type of proportional representation would be to mandate proportionate shares of electoral votes based on candidates' popular vote totals. But if this system were adopted, there would be no need to retain the electoral college and go through the charade of a phony election; the result could be achieved with phantom electoral votes. The advantages of such a plan are the advantages of proportional representation: principally that it lessens the likelihood of a loser of the popular vote winning the electoral vote. But it does not eliminate that possibility; it merely lessens it.

Another option seeks to compromise between winner-take-all and proportionality. The so-called national bonus plan calls for adding a fixed number of electoral votes to the existing electoral college total of the candidate with the most popular votes nationwide.[24] This plan would reduce the chance of deadlock, but it would not eliminate it. Moreover, in a close three-way race, the bonus would vastly magnify the electoral votes of a candidate who receives a bare plurality of the popular vote but who could still be the popular majority's *third* choice. The electoral college has been criticized for permitting the victory of the "wrong winner"—the popular majority's second choice who nonetheless commands a majority in the electoral college. Yet the national bonus plan poses similar possibilities in a three-way race.

Although seldom identified as such, the purest form of proportional representation is one person, one vote. In the context of presidential election, this would mean direct popular election. It would present several problems, however.

One is the chaos and potential for electoral fraud that could ensue in a close election. Direct popular election could create demands for a national recount in an election such as that of 1960, where the candidates were separated by only 115,000 votes. The results of prolonged uncertainty could be disastrous. Alexander Bickel suggested that the outcome in such an election is really a standoff. In such circumstances, he contended, it is more important that the system decide quickly than that it decide accurately.[25] It is true that one does not consider flipping a coin when gubernatorial or Senate elections are close; one recounts and keeps recounting until the mathematical victor can be identified. Why should the presidency be any different? Perhaps because the hole in government would be much greater if the presidency were undetermined for six months than if a governorship or Senate seat remained open. It might be said, too, that the electoral college is not immune to the danger of a close election and prolonged recount or to fraud. Still, the electoral college system has worked without a hitch in producing clear winners for 168 years. For some reason, the parade of potential disasters painted by its critics has yet to materialize.

Another problem is that direct election could necessitate a runoff election, or some preferential ballot system, when a third-party or independent candidate is involved. This is the only way to ensure that the new president is the majority's first choice in the event no candidate receives a majority in the general election (this has occurred fifteen times in American history). Runoff elections have the advantage of familiarity, as they are fairly common and well accepted in state elections. As an alternative, a preferential ballot might require indication of a voter's second choice, with votes cast for the candidate who finishes third reallocated to the voter's second-choice candidate. (For this so-called single transferrable vote, the tabulations would be made on the same day, thereby avoiding the need for a runoff.)

But each approach would represent a radical change in the culture of presidential elections—so drastic, perhaps, as to undermine their acceptance. In addition, if the runoff option were selected, it would be necessary to specify a cutoff level. One might believe, for example, that a runoff should not have been required in all fifteen elections in which a "minority" president was elected; perhaps a candidate receiving, say, the greatest margin over 40 percent of the vote should be deemed the winner. Had this system been in effect from the beginning, only one runoff election would have been required—for Abraham Lincoln (who received 39.8 percent of the popular vote in 1860).

Finally, a system of direct election would likely effect a pernicious change in campaign tactics. It would focus candidates' attention and money on urban and suburban areas, where votes are concentrated and where media outlets—primarily television—provide more bang for the buck. Fine, one might say; let the market rule. But, as a result, large segments of the population would likely be ignored. Their participation and interest would nosedive. It has been said that it is less important what books a people read than that they read the same books. The same principle applies here: it is important that members of a society have common political reference points—that they hear the same speeches and see the same political commercials. Empathy is impossible without shared information or experience. A nation of one people cannot be achieved by encouraging presidential campaigns comprised of narrowly tailored television spots targeted at precisely identified subgroups. But it can be achieved by providing the incentive to run national campaigns directed at all of the American people.

For these reasons, states should be encouraged to adopt the district system, recently a topic of renewed interest. In 1992, Florida considered and rejected the district system. Proposals to move to the district system also were introduced in Arizona, Connecticut, Georgia, Louisiana, New Jersey, North Carolina, and Virginia. James Madison believed that it was that system that was contemplated by the Framers of the Constitution.[26] Under the winner-take-all system in effect in forty-eight states, presidential candidates largely ignore states where victory is all but certain or all but impossible. Campaign resources are sunk into "battleground" states. The upshot is, again, that only a privileged segment of the electorate participates in the national political dialogue every four years. Moving to the district system, however, would not necessarily involve all voters in that dialogue. It would still be more expensive to reach some than others; $3 million spent on Los Angeles television spots that are beamed to four congressional districts might provide more "bang for the buck" than the same amount spent on one congressional district in western Montana. Still, the district system would lessen such disparities. A candidate who would write off the entire state of winner-take-all California might, if given the district-by-district option, target Orange County or San Francisco. The district system would compel presidential candidates to speak to the electorate in each congressional district; none would count for more than another. Moreover, the district system would resuscitate local party organizations by encouraging district-based, grass-roots campaigns without further disaggregating power, as the district system also would encourage broad-based national campaigns aimed at nationally dispersed voters falling within the same demographic strata. Finally, if the district system were adopted nationwide, presidential candidates' electoral votes would correlate more closely with their popular votes. Consequently, the general election winner would be less likely to be a loser in the general election.

States cannot be compelled to adopt the district system. Under the Constitution, they are assigned the power to select the system by which their electors will be selected. But Congress can, constitutionally, enact legislation rewarding states that adopt such a law or penalizing those that do not. For example, in 1984 it did just this when it directed the withholding of federal highway funds from states permitting the purchase of alcohol by persons under the age of twenty-one—a law upheld by the Supreme Court in *South Dakota v. Dole* (1987).[27] There is a federal interest in maintaining the integrity of presidential elections. It would seem consistent with that interest to, say, provide states that have adopted the district system with financial assistance to carry out elections.

Conclusion

There is no perfect electoral system. No system is immune to manipulation. Every system can produce unintended results. The American system has its full share of flaws. "There are objections," Madison wrote, "against every mode that has been, or perhaps can be proposed." [28] But the issue is not absolute merit. It is comparative merit, and the comparison is with an alternative or alternatives that will undoubtedly have unforeseeable effects that will reverberate through the political system. This is why John F. Kennedy opposed abolition of the electoral college. "It is not only the unit vote for the Presidency we are talking about," he said, "but a whole solar system of governmental power. If it is proposed to change the balance of power of one of the elements of the solar system, it is necessary to consider the others." [29]

The literature is rife with innumerable "solutions" to the electoral college "problem." They range from abolition (with direct election of the president) to retention (with electors added to reflect the outcome of the popular vote results[30]). And there are a variety of solutions in between. One would assign a state's electoral votes proportionately. Another would do so with "phantom" electoral votes, the real electors having been eliminated. Yet another would award them all to the candidate winning the state's popular vote.

Too often the putative reformers ignore the rest of the political solar system. They would do better to work backward, asking first what goal they seek to achieve by changing the system. The objective, or value sought to be advanced, will determine the means. For example, is the principal objective enhanced legitimacy? If so, direct election might be the preferred route. Direct election would make it impossible for a loser in the general election to win in the electoral college as occurred in the election of John Quincy Adams in 1824, Rutherford B. Hayes in 1876, and Grover Cleveland in 1888. Or is the objective enhanced power for minorities? If so, one would opt for a winner-take-all system in the selection of electors rather than a district system.

Similarly, the means will vary if the objective is to reinforce values of federalism or of separation of powers, or if the objective is to bring more voters into the national political dialogue, or to lessen the danger of a national recount, or to strengthen (or weaken) the two-party system, or to pick better presidents. Each of the proposed reforms has ramifications for all of these elements of the political solar system.

What, for example, are the systemic effects of moving to a system of direct election of the president? Would it lessen the power of states by eliminating an institution—the electoral college—that recognizes their electoral identity? Many have commented on the tendency of the electoral college to favor small states (each state is entitled to three electoral votes regardless of its size, violating the one person, one vote precept). Is this a countervailing advantage worth saving? If not—if the electoral college should be abolished for this reason—does not the same objection apply to retention of the Senate? Would direct election weaken the power of minorities? Is this what is wanted? Would it encourage recounts and fraud? What would be the rationale for continuing with national nominating conventions—would it not make sense to move to a national primary system? How would a national primary system affect state political parties? If it weakened state political parties, how would that affect congressional elections in that state? Would special interests and their political action committees move to fill in the vacuum? If so, how would that affect the composition of Congress and congressional power vis-à-vis the presidency? For that matter, would a nationally elected president not gain power in relation to Congress with the claim that he or she is the only elected official of *all* the people?

No one is prescient enough to be able to predict the ultimate structural results of fundamental change in the presidential election system. Thus, it is not simply disagreement on the objective. It is a well-founded uncertainty about the effects throughout the "solar system" that produced disagreement in Philadelphia in 1787 and continues to this day to prevent the formation of a national consensus. One would be wise to recall the words of Alexander Bickel: "There are great virtues in a conservative attitude towards structural features of government. The sudden abandonment of institutions is an act that reverberates in ways no one can predict and many come to regret." [31]

The danger in tinkering with the current system of presidential election to make it less republican is that, the best efforts notwithstanding, it could emerge less republican *and* less democratic.

NOTES

1. James S. Fishkin, *Democracy and Deliberation* (New Haven, Conn.: Yale University Press, 1991), 95.
2. *Williams v. Rhodes,* 393 U.S. 23 (1968).
3. The cases that follow were compiled by the U.S. Library of Congress, Congressional Research Service, in Thomas M. Durbin, "The Electoral College Method of Electing the President and Vice President and Proposals for Reform," memorandum, Washington, D.C., August 8, 1988, 17-18.
4. *McCarthy v. Tribbitt,* 421 F. Supp. 1193 (D. Del. 1976).
5. *McCarthy v. Askew,* 420 F. Supp. 775 (S.D. Fla. 1976), *aff'd* 540 F. 2d 1254 (5th Cir. 1976).
6. *McCarthy v. Andrus,* No. C-1-76-191 (D. Idaho 1976).
7. *McCarthy v. Lunding,* No. 76-C-2733 (N.D. Ill. 1976).

8. *McCarthy v. Shanahan*, No. C-76-237-C6 (D. Kan. 1976).

9. *McCarthy v. Austin*, 423 F. Supp. 990 (W.D. Mich. 1976).

10. *McCarthy v. Kirkpatrick*, 420 F. Supp. 366 (W.D. Mo. 1976).

11. *McCarthy v. Exon*, 424 F. Supp. 1143 (D. Neb. 1976), *aff'd* 429 U.S. 972 (1976).

12. *McCarthy v. Evans*, No. Civ.-76-565P (D. N.M. 1976).

13. *McCarthy v. Slater*, 535 P. 2d 489 (D. Okla. 1976).

14. *McCarthy v. Briscoe*, 418 F. Supp. 816 (W.D. Texas 1976), *app. denied* 539 F. 2d 1353 (5th Cir. 1976), *app. denied* 429 U.S. 1317 (1976).

15. *McCarthy v. Rampton*, No. C-76-303 (D.C. Utah 1976).

16. *Anderson v. Firestone*, 499 F. Supp. 1027 (N.D. Fla. 1980).

17. *Anderson v. Mills*, 497 F. Supp. 283 (E.D. Ky. 1980), *aff'd* 664 F.2d 602 (6th Cir. 1981).

18. *Anderson v. Quinn*, 495 F. Supp. 730 (D. Maine 1980), *aff'd* 636 F. 2d 616 (1st Cir. 1980).

19. *Anderson v. Morris*, 500 F. Supp. 778 (D. Md. 1980), *aff'd* 636 F. 2d 616 (4th Cir. 1980).

20. *Anderson v. Hooper*, 498 F. Supp. 898 (D. N.M. 1980).

21. *Anderson v. Babb*, No. 80-561-CIV-5 (E.D. N.C. 1980), *aff'd* 632 F. 2d 300 (4th Cir. 1980).

22. *Anderson v. Celebrezee*, 449 F. Supp. 121 (S.D. Oh. 1980), *rev'd* 664 F. 2d 554 (6th Cir. 1980), *rev'd* 460 U.S. 780 (1980).

23. *Anderson v. Babb*, No. 80-561-CIV-5 (E.D. N.C. 1980) at 30.

24. Twentieth Century Fund, *Winner Take All: Report of the Twentieth Century Fund Task Force on Reform of the Presidential Election Process* (New York: Holmes & Meier, 1978).

25. Alexander M. Bickel, *Reform and Continuity* (New York: Harper Colophon Books, 1971), 31-33.

26. *McPherson v. Blacker*, 146 U.S. 1 (1892) at 27.

27. *South Dakota v. Dole*, 483 U.S. 203 (1987).

28. Max Farrand, ed., *The Records of the Federal Convention of 1787*, Vol. 3 (New Haven, Conn.: Yale University Press, 1937), 77.

29. U.S. Congress, Senate, *Congressional Record*, daily ed., 84th Cong., 2d sess., March 20, 1956, S150.

30. Neil R. Pierce and Lawrence D. Longley, *The People's President: The Electoral College in American History and the Direct Vote Alternative* (New Haven: Yale University Press, 1981), 172-177.

31. Quoted in Alexander Bickel, "Comment," *New Republic*, May 7, 1977, 5.

Appendixes:

Documents Related to the Electoral College

Appendix A

Constitution of
the United States

We the People of the United States, in Order to form a more perfect
Union, establish Justice, insure domestic Tranquility, provide for
the common defence, promote the general Welfare, and secure the
Blessings of Liberty to ourselves and our Posterity, do ordain and
establish this Constitution for the United States of America.

Article I

Section 1. All legislative Powers herein granted shall be vested in
a Congress of the United States, which shall consist of a Senate and
House of Representatives.

Section 2. The House of Representatives shall be composed of
Members chosen every second Year by the People of the several
States, and the Electors in each State shall have the Qualifications
requisite for Electors of the most numerous Branch of the State
Legislature.

No Person shall be a Representative who shall not have attained
to the age of twenty five Years, and been seven Years a Citizen of the
United States, and who shall not, when elected, be an Inhabitant of
that State in which he shall be chosen.

[Representatives and direct Taxes shall be apportioned among the
several States which may be included within this Union, according to
their respective Numbers, which shall be determined by adding to
the whole Number of free Persons, including those bound to Service
for a Term of Years, and excluding Indians not taxed, three fifths of
all other Persons.][1] The actual Enumeration shall be made within

---

The provisions of the Constitution that pertain to the president and vice president
are italicized.

three Years after the first Meeting of the Congress of the United States, and within every subsequent Term of ten Years, in such Manner as they shall by Law direct. The Number of Representatives shall not exceed one for every thirty Thousand, but each State shall have at Least one Representative; and until such enumeration shall be made, the State of New Hampshire shall be entitled to chuse three, Massachusetts eight, Rhode-Island and Providence Plantations one, Connecticut five, New-York six, New Jersey four, Pennsylvania eight, Delaware one, Maryland six, Virginia ten, North Carolina five, South Carolina five, and Georgia three.

When vacancies happen in the Representation from any State, the Executive Authority thereof shall issue Writs of Election to fill such Vacancies.

The House of Representatives shall chuse their Speaker and other Officers; and shall have the sole Power of Impeachment.

Section 3. The Senate of the United States shall be composed of two Senators from each State, [chosen by the Legislature thereof,][2] for six Years; and each Senator shall have one Vote.

Immediately after they shall be assembled in Consequence of the first Election, they shall be divided as equally as may be into three Classes. The Seats of the Senators of the first Class shall be vacated at the Expiration of the second Year, of the second Class at the Expiration of the fourth Year, and of the third Class at the Expiration of the sixth Year, so that one third may be chosen every second Year; [and if Vacancies happen by Resignation, or otherwise, during the Recess of the Legislature of any State, the Executive thereof may make temporary Appointments until the next Meeting of the Legislature, which shall then fill such Vacancies.][3]

No Person shall be a Senator who shall not have attained to the Age of thirty Years, and been nine Years a Citizen of the United States, and who shall not, when elected, be an Inhabitant of that State for which he shall be chosen.

The Vice President of the United States shall be President of the Senate, but shall have no Vote, unless they be equally divided.

The Senate shall chuse their other Officers, and also a President pro tempore, in the Absence of the Vice President, or when he shall exercise the Office of President of the United States.

The Senate shall have the sole Power to try all Impeachments. When sitting for that Purpose, they shall be on Oath or Affirmation. When the President of the United States is tried, the Chief Justice shall preside: And no Person shall be convicted without the Concurrence of two thirds of the Members present.

Judgment in Cases of Impeachment shall not extend further than to removal from Office, and disqualification to hold and enjoy any Office of honor, Trust or Profit under the United States: but the Party convicted shall nevertheless be liable and subject to Indictment, Trial, Judgment and Punishment, according to Law.

Section 4. The Times, Places and Manner of holding Elections for Senators and Representatives, shall be prescribed in each State by the Legislature thereof; but the Congress may at any time by Law make or alter such Regulations, except as to the Places of chusing Senators.

The Congress shall assemble at least once in every Year, and such Meeting shall [be on the first Monday in December],[4] unless they shall by Law appoint a different Day.

Section 5. Each House shall be the Judge of the Elections, Returns and Qualifications of its own Members, and a Majority of each shall constitute a Quorum to do Business; but a smaller Number may adjourn from day to day, and may be authorized to compel the Attendance of absent Members, in such Manner, and under such Penalties as each House may provide.

Each House may determine the Rules of its Proceedings, punish its Members for disorderly Behaviour, and, with the Concurrence of two thirds, expel a Member.

Each House shall keep a Journal of its Proceedings, and from time to time publish the same, excepting such Parts as may in their Judgment require Secrecy; and the Yeas and Nays of the Members of either House on any question shall, at the Desire of one fifth of those Present, be entered on the Journal.

Neither House, during the Session of Congress, shall, without the Consent of the other, adjourn for more than three days, nor to any other Place than that in which the two Houses shall be sitting.

Section 6. The Senators and Representatives shall receive a Compensation for their Services, to be ascertained by Law, and paid out of the Treasury of the United States. They shall in all Cases, except Treason, Felony and Breach of the Peace, be privileged from Arrest during their Attendance at the Session of their respective Houses, and in going to and returning from the same; and for any Speech or Debate in either House, they shall not be questioned in any other Place.

No Senator or Representative shall, during the Time for which he was elected, be appointed to any civil Office under the Authority of the United States, which shall have been created, or the Emoluments whereof shall have been encreased during such time; and no Person holding any Office under the United States, shall be a Member of either House during his Continuance in Office.

Section 7. All Bills for raising Revenue shall originate in the House of Representatives; but the Senate may propose or concur with Amendments as on other Bills.

Every Bill which shall have passed the House of Representatives and the Senate, shall, before it become a Law, be presented to the President of the United States; If he approve he shall sign it, but if not he shall return it, with his Objections to that House in which it shall have originated, who shall enter the Objections at large on their Journal, and proceed to reconsider it. If after such Reconsideration two thirds of that House shall agree to pass the Bill, it shall be sent, together with the Objections, to the other House, by which it shall likewise be reconsidered, and if approved by two thirds of that House, it shall become a Law. But in all such Cases the Votes of both Houses shall be determined by yeas and Nays, and the Names of the Persons voting for and against the Bill shall be entered on the Journal of each House respectively. If any Bill shall not be returned by the President within ten Days (Sundays excepted) after it shall have been presented to him, the Same shall be a Law, in like Manner as if he had signed it, unless the Congress by their Adjournment prevent its Return, in which Case it shall not be a Law.

Every Order, Resolution, or Vote to which the Concurrence of the Senate and House of Representatives may be necessary (except on a question of Adjournment) shall be presented to the President of the United States; and before the Same shall take Effect, shall be approved by him, or being disapproved by him, shall be repassed by two thirds of the Senate and House of Representatives, according to the Rules and Limitations prescribed in the Case of a Bill.

Section 8. The Congress shall have Power To lay and collect Taxes, Duties, Imposts and Excises, to pay the Debts and provide for the common Defence and general Welfare of the United States; but all Duties, Imposts and Excises shall be uniform throughout the United States;

To borrow Money on the credit of the United States;

To regulate Commerce with foreign Nations, and among the several States, and with the Indian Tribes;

To establish an uniform Rule of Naturalization, and uniform Laws on the subject of Bankruptcies throughout the United States;

To coin Money, regulate the Value thereof, and of foreign Coin, and fix the Standard of Weights and Measures;

To provide for the Punishment of counterfeiting the Securities and current Coin of the United States;

To establish Post Offices and post Roads;

To promote the Progress of Science and useful Arts, by securing for limited Times to Authors and Inventors the exclusive Right to their respective Writings and Discoveries;

To constitute Tribunals inferior to the supreme Court;

To define and punish Piracies and Felonies committed on the high Seas, and Offences against the Law of Nations;

To declare War, grant Letters of Marque and Reprisal, and make Rules concerning Captures on Land and Water;

To raise and support Armies, but no Appropriation of Money to that Use shall be for a longer Term than two Years;

To provide and maintain a Navy;

To make Rules for the Government and Regulation of the land and naval Forces;

To provide for calling forth the Militia to execute the Laws of the Union, suppress Insurrections and repel Invasions;

To provide for organizing, arming, and disciplining, the Militia, and for governing such Part of them as may be employed in the Service of the United States, reserving to the States respectively, the Appointment of the Officers, and the Authority of training the Militia according to the discipline prescribed by Congress;

To exercise exclusive Legislation in all Cases whatsoever, over such District (not exceeding ten Miles square) as may, by Cession of particular States, and the Acceptance of Congress, become the Seat of the Government of the United States, and to exercise like Authority over all Places purchased by the Consent of the Legislature of the State in which the Same shall be, for the Erection of Forts, Magazines, Arsenals, dock-Yards, and other needful Buildings; —And

To make all Laws which shall be necessary and proper for carrying into Execution the foregoing Powers, and all other Powers vested by this Constitution in the Government of the United States, or in any Department or Officer thereof.

Section 9. The Migration or Importation of such Persons as any of the States now existing shall think proper to admit, shall not be prohibited by the Congress prior to the Year one thousand eight hundred and eight, but a Tax or duty may be imposed on such Importation, not exceeding ten dollars for each Person.

The Privilege of the Writ of Habeas Corpus shall not be suspended, unless when in Cases of Rebellion or Invasion the public Safety may require it.

No Bill of Attainder or ex post facto Law shall be passed.

No Capitation, or other direct, Tax shall be laid, unless in Proportion to the Census or Enumeration herein before directed to be taken.[5]

No Tax or Duty shall be laid on Articles exported from any State.

No Preference shall be given by any Regulation of Commerce or Revenue to the Ports of one State over those of another; nor shall Vessels bound to, or from, one State, be obliged to enter, clear, or pay Duties in another.

No Money shall be drawn from the Treasury, but in Consequence of Appropriations made by Law; and a regular Statement and Account of the Receipts and Expenditures of all public Money shall be published from time to time.

No Title of Nobility shall be granted by the United States: And no Person holding any Office of Profit or Trust under them, shall, without the Consent of the Congress, accept of any present, Emolument, Office, or Title, of any kind whatever, from any King, Prince, or foreign State.

Section 10. No State shall enter into any Treaty, Alliance, or Confederation; grant Letters of Marque and Reprisal; coin Money; emit Bills of Credit; make any Thing but gold and silver Coin a Tender in Payment of Debts; pass any Bill of Attainder, ex post facto Law, or Law impairing the Obligation of Contracts, or grant any Title of Nobility.

No State shall, without the Consent of the Congress, lay any Imposts or Duties on Imports or Exports, except what may be absolutely necessary for executing it's inspection Laws: and the net Produce of all Duties and Imposts, laid by any State on Imports or Exports, shall be for the Use of the Treasury of the United States; and all such Laws shall be subject to the Revision and Controul of the Congress.

No State shall, without the Consent of Congress, lay any Duty of Tonnage, keep Troops, or Ships of War in time of Peace, enter into any Agreement or Compact with another State, or with a foreign Power, or engage in War, unless actually invaded, or in such imminent Danger as will not admit of delay.

Article II

Section 1. *The executive Power shall be vested in a President of the United States of America. He shall hold his Office during the Term of four Years, and, together with the Vice President, chosen for the same Term, be elected, as follows*

Each State shall appoint, in such Manner as the Legislature thereof may direct, a Number of Electors, equal to the whole Number of Senators and Representatives to which the State may be entitled in the Congress: but no Senator or Representative, or Person holding an Office of Trust or Profit under the United States, shall be appointed an Elector.

[The Electors shall meet in their respective States, and vote by Ballot for two Persons, of whom one at least shall not be an Inhabitant of the same State with themselves. And they shall make a List of all the Persons voted for, and of the Number of Votes for each; which List they shall sign and certify, and transmit sealed to the Seat of the Government of the United States, directed to the President of the Senate. The President of the Senate shall, in the Presence of the Senate and House of Representatives, open all the Certificates, and the Votes shall then be counted. The Person having the greatest Number of Votes shall be the President, if such Number be a Majority of the whole Number of Electors appointed; and if there be more than one who have such Majority, and have an equal Number of Votes, then the House of Representatives shall immediately chuse by Ballot one of them for President; and if no Person have a Majority, then from the five highest on the list the said House shall in like Manner chuse the President. But in chusing the President, the Votes shall be taken by States, the Representation from each State having one Vote; A quorum for this Purpose shall consist of a Member or Members from two thirds of the States, and a Majority of all the States shall be necessary to a Choice. In every Case, after the Choice of the President, the Person having the greatest Number of Votes of the Electors shall be the Vice President.

But if there should remain two or more who have equal Votes, the Senate shall chuse from them by Ballot the Vice President.][6]

The Congress may determine the Time of chusing the Electors, and the Day on which they shall give their Votes; which Day shall be the same throughout the United States.

No Person except a natural born Citizen, or a Citizen of the United States, at the time of the Adoption of this Constitution, shall be eligible to the Office of President; neither shall any Person be eligible to that Office who shall not have attained to the Age of thirty five Years, and been fourteen Years a Resident within the United States.

In Case of the Removal of the President from Office, or of his Death, Resignation, or Inability to discharge the Powers and Duties of the said Office,[7] the Same shall devolve on the Vice President, and the Congress may by Law provide for the Case of Removal, Death, Resignation or Inability, both of the President and Vice President, declaring what Officer shall then act as President, and such Officer shall act accordingly, until the Disability be removed, or a President shall be elected.

The President shall, at stated Times, receive for his Services, a Compensation, which shall neither be encreased nor diminished during the Period for which he shall have been elected, and he shall not receive within that Period any other Emolument from the United States, or any of them.

Before he enter on the Execution of his Office, he shall take the following Oath or Affirmation:—"I do solemnly swear (or affirm) that I will faithfully execute the Office of President of the United States, and will to the best of my Ability, preserve, protect and defend the Constitution of the United States."

Section 2. The President shall be Commander in Chief of the Army and Navy of the United States, and of the Militia of the several States, when called into the actual Service of the United States; he may require the Opinion, in writing, of the principal Officer in each of the executive Departments, upon any Subject relating to the Duties of their respective Offices, and he shall have Power to grant Reprieves and Pardons for Offences against the United States, except in Cases of Impeachment.

He shall have Power, by and with the Advice and Consent of the Senate, to make Treaties, provided two thirds of the Senators present concur; and he shall nominate, and by and with the Advice and

Consent of the Senate, shall appoint Ambassadors, other public Ministers and Consuls, Judges of the supreme Court, and all other Officers of the United States, whose Appointments are not herein otherwise provided for, and which shall be established by Law: but the Congress may by Law vest the Appointment of such inferior Officers, as they think proper, in the President alone, in the Courts of Law, or in the Heads of Departments.

The President shall have Power to fill up all Vacancies that may happen during the Recess of the Senate, by granting Commissions which shall expire at the End of their next Session.

Section 3. He shall from time to time give to the Congress Information of the State of the Union, and recommend to their Consideration such Measures as he shall judge necessary and expedient; he may, on extraordinary Occasions, convene both Houses, or either of them, and in Case of Disagreement between them, with Respect to the Time of Adjournment, he may adjourn them to such Time as he shall think proper; he shall receive Ambassadors and other public Ministers; he shall take Care that the Laws be faithfully executed, and shall Commission all the Officers of the United States.

Section 4. The President, Vice President and all civil Officers of the United States, shall be removed from Office on Impeachment for, and Conviction of, Treason, Bribery, or other high Crimes and Misdemeanors.

Article III

Section 1. The judicial Power of the United States, shall be vested in one supreme Court, and in such inferior Courts as the Congress may from time to time ordain and establish. The Judges, both of the supreme and inferior Courts, shall hold their Offices during good Behaviour, and shall, at stated Times, receive for their Services, a Compensation, which shall not be diminished during their Continuance in Office.

Section 2. The judicial Power shall extend to all Cases, in Law and Equity, arising under this Constitution, the Laws of the United States, and Treaties made, or which shall be made, under their Authority; — to all Cases affecting Ambassadors, other public Ministers and Consuls; — to all Cases of admiralty and maritime Jurisdiction; — to Controversies to which the United States shall be a Party; — to Controversies between two or more States; — between a State and Citizens of another State;[8] — between Citizens of different States; — between Citizens of the same State claiming Lands under Grants of different States, and between a State, or the Citizens thereof, and foreign States, Citizens or Subjects.[8]

In all Cases affecting Ambassadors, other public Ministers and Consuls, and those in which a State shall be Party, the supreme Court shall have original Jurisdiction. In all the other Cases before mentioned, the supreme Court shall have appellate Jurisdiction, both as to Law and Fact, with such Exceptions, and under such Regulations as the Congress shall make.

The Trial of all Crimes, except in Cases of Impeachment, shall be by Jury; and such Trial shall be held in the State where the said Crimes shall have been committed; but when not committed within any State, the Trial shall be at such Place or Places as the Congress may by Law have directed.

Section 3. Treason against the United States, shall consist only in levying War against them, or in adhering to their Enemies, giving them Aid and Comfort. No Person shall be convicted of Treason unless on the Testimony of two Witnesses to the same overt Act, or on Confession in open Court.

The Congress shall have Power to declare the Punishment of Treason, but no Attainder of Treason shall work Corruption of Blood, or Forfeiture except during the Life of the Person attainted.

Article IV

Section 1. Full Faith and Credit shall be given in each State to the public Acts, Records, and judicial Proceedings of every other State. And the Congress may by general Laws prescribe the Manner in which such Acts, Records and Proceedings shall be proved, and the Effect thereof.

Section 2. The Citizens of each State shall be entitled to all Privileges and Immunities of Citizens in the several States.

A Person charged in any State with Treason, Felony, or other Crime, who shall flee from Justice, and be found in another State, shall on Demand of the executive Authority of the State from which he fled, be delivered up, to be removed to the State having Jurisdiction of the Crime.

[No Person held to Service or Labour in one State, under the

Laws thereof, escaping into another, shall, in Consequence of any Law or Regulation therein, be discharged from such Service or Labour, but shall be delivered up on Claim of the Party to whom such Service or Labour may be due.]⁹

Section 3. New States may be admitted by the Congress into this Union; but no new State shall be formed or erected within the Jurisdiction of any other State; nor any State be formed by the Junction of two or more States, or Parts of States, without the Consent of the Legislatures of the States concerned as well as of the Congress.

The Congress shall have Power to dispose of and make all needful Rules and Regulations respecting the Territory or other Property belonging to the United States; and nothing in this Constitution shall be so construed as to Prejudice any Claims of the United States, or of any particular State.

Section 4. The United States shall guarantee to every State in this Union a Republican Form of Government, and shall protect each of them against Invasion; and on Application of the Legislature, or of the Executive (when the Legislature cannot be convened) against domestic Violence.

Article V

The Congress, whenever two thirds of both Houses shall deem it necessary, shall propose Amendments to this Constitution, or, on the Application of the Legislatures of two thirds of the several States, shall call a Convention for proposing Amendments, which, in either Case, shall be valid to all Intents and Purposes, as Part of this Constitution, when ratified by the Legislatures of three fourths of the several States, or by Conventions in three fourths thereof, as the one or the other Mode of Ratification may be proposed by the Congress; Provided [that no Amendment which may be made prior to the Year One thousand eight hundred and eight shall in any Manner affect the first and fourth Clauses in the Ninth Section of the first Article; and]¹⁰ that no State, without its Consent, shall be deprived of its equal Suffrage in the Senate.

Article VI

All Debts contracted and Engagements entered into, before the Adoption of this Constitution, shall be as valid against the United

States under this Constitution, as under the Confederation.

This Constitution, and the Laws of the United States which shall be made in Pursuance thereof; and all Treaties made, or which shall be made, under the Authority of the United States, shall be the supreme Law of the Land; and the Judges in every State shall be bound thereby, any Thing in the Constitution or Laws of any State to the Contrary notwithstanding.

The Senators and Representatives before mentioned, and the Members of the several State Legislatures, and all executive and judicial Officers, both of the United States and of the several States, shall be bound by Oath or Affirmation, to support this Constitution; but no religious Test shall ever be required as a Qualification to any Office or public Trust under the United States.

Article VII

The Ratification of the Conventions of nine States, shall be sufficient for the Establishment of this Constitution between the States so ratifying the Same.

Done in Convention by the Unanimous Consent of the States present the Seventeenth Day of September in the Year of our Lord one thousand seven hundred and Eighty seven and of the Independence of the United States of America the Twelfth. IN WITNESS whereof We have hereunto subscribed our Names,

George Washington,
President and
deputy from Virginia.

New Hampshire:	John Langdon, Nicholas Gilman.
Massachusetts:	Nathaniel Gorham, Rufus King.
Connecticut:	William Samuel Johnson, Roger Sherman.
New York:	Alexander Hamilton.
New Jersey:	William Livingston, David Brearley, William Paterson, Jonathan Dayton.

Pennsylvania:

Benjamin Franklin,
Thomas Mifflin,
Robert Morris,
George Clymer,
Thomas FitzSimons,
Jared Ingersoll,
James Wilson,
Gouverneur Morris.

Delaware:

George Read,
Gunning Bedford Jr.,
John Dickinson,
Richard Bassett,
Jacob Broom.

Maryland:

James McHenry,
Daniel of St. Thomas Jenifer,
Daniel Carroll.

Virginia:

John Blair,
James Madison Jr.

North Carolina:

William Blount,
Richard Dobbs Spaight,
Hugh Williamson.

South Carolina:

John Rutledge,
Charles Cotesworth Pinckney,
Charles Pinckney,
Pierce Butler.

Georgia:

William Few,
Abraham Baldwin.

[The language of the original Constitution, not including the Amendments, was adopted by a convention of the states on September 17, 1787, and was subsequently ratified by the states on the following dates: Delaware, December 7, 1787; Pennsylvania, December 12, 1787; New Jersey, December 18, 1787; Georgia, January 2, 1788; Connecticut, January 9, 1788; Massachusetts, February 6, 1788; Maryland, April 28, 1788; South Carolina, May 23, 1788; New Hampshire, June 21, 1788.

Ratification was completed on June 21, 1788.

The Constitution subsequently was ratified by Virginia, June 25, 1788; New York, July 26, 1788; North Carolina, November 21, 1789; Rhode Island, May 29, 1790; and Vermont, January 10, 1791.]

Amendments

Amendment I

[First ten amendments ratified December 15, 1791.]

Congress shall make no law respecting an establishment of religion, or prohibiting the free exercise thereof; or abridging the freedom of speech, or of the press; or the right of the people peaceably to assemble, and to petition the Government for a redress of grievances.

Amendment II

A well regulated Militia, being necessary to the security of a free State, the right of the people to keep and bear Arms, shall not be infringed.

Amendment III

No Soldier shall, in time of peace be quartered in any house, without the consent of the Owner, nor in time of war, but in a manner to be prescribed by law.

Amendment IV

The right of the people to be secure in their persons, houses, papers, and effects, against unreasonable searches and seizures, shall not be violated, and no Warrants shall issue, but upon probable cause, supported by Oath or affirmation, and particularly describing the place to be searched, and the persons or things to be seized.

Amendment V

No person shall be held to answer for a capital, or otherwise infamous crime, unless on a presentment or indictment of a Grand Jury, except in cases arising in the land or naval forces, or in the Militia, when in actual service in time of War or public danger; nor shall any person be subject for the same offence to be twice put in jeopardy of life or limb; nor shall be compelled in any criminal case to be a witness against himself, nor be deprived of life, liberty, or property, without due process of law; nor shall private property be taken for public use, without just compensation.

Amendment VI

In all criminal prosecutions, the accused shall enjoy the right to a speedy and public trial, by an impartial jury of the State and district wherein the crime shall have been committed, which district shall have been previously ascertained by law, and to be informed of the nature and cause of the accusation; to be confronted with the witnesses against him; to have compulsory process for obtaining witnesses in his favor, and to have the Assistance of Counsel for his defence.

Amendment VII

In Suits at common law, where the value in controversy shall exceed twenty dollars, the right of trial by jury shall be preserved, and no fact tried by a jury, shall be otherwise re-examined in any Court of the United States, than according to the rules of the common law.

Amendment VIII

Excessive bail shall not be required, nor excessive fines imposed, nor cruel and unusual punishments inflicted.

Amendment IX

The enumeration in the Constitution, of certain rights, shall not be construed to deny or disparage others retained by the people.

Amendment X

The powers not delegated to the United States by the Constitution, nor prohibited by it to the States, are reserved to the States respectively, or to the people.

Amendment XI [Ratified February 7, 1795]

The Judicial power of the United States shall not be construed to extend to any suit in law or equity, commenced or prosecuted against one of the United States by Citizens of another State, or by Citizens or Subjects of any Foreign State.

Amendment XII *[Ratified June 15, 1804]*

The Electors shall meet in their respective states and vote by ballot for President and Vice-President, one of whom, at least, shall not be an inhabitant of the same state with themselves; they shall name in their ballots the person voted for as President, and in distinct ballots the person voted for as Vice-President, and they shall make distinct lists of all persons voted for as President, and of all persons voted for as Vice-President, and of the number of votes for each, which lists they shall sign and certify, and transmit sealed to the seat of the government of the United States, directed to the President of the Senate; — The President of the Senate shall, in the presence of the Senate and House of Representatives, open all the certificates and the votes shall then be counted; — The person having the greatest number of votes for President, shall be the President, if such number be a majority of the whole number of Electors appointed; and if no person have such majority, then from the persons having the highest numbers not exceeding three on the list of those voted for as President, the House of Representatives shall choose immediately, by ballot, the President. But in choosing the President, the votes shall be taken by states, the representation from each state having one vote; a quorum for this purpose shall consist of a member or members from two-thirds of the states, and a majority of all the states shall be necessary to a choice. *[And if the House of Representatives shall not choose a President whenever the right of choice shall devolve upon them, before the fourth day of March next following, then the Vice-President shall act as President, as in the case of the death or other constitutional disability of the President. —]*[11] The person having the greatest number of votes as Vice-President, shall be the Vice-President, if such number be a majority of the whole number of Electors appointed, and if no person have a majority, then from the two highest numbers on the list, the Senate shall choose the Vice-President; a quorum for the purpose shall consist of two-thirds of the whole number of Senators, and a majority of the whole number shall be necessary to a choice. But no person constitutionally ineligible to the office of President shall be eligible to that of Vice-President of the United States.

Amendment XIII [Ratified December 6, 1865]

Section 1. Neither slavery nor involuntary servitude, except as a punishment for crime whereof the party shall have been duly convicted, shall exist within the United States, or any place subject to their jurisdiction.

Section 2. Congress shall have power to enforce this article by appropriate legislation.

Amendment XIV [Ratified July 9, 1868]

Section 1. All persons born or naturalized in the United States, and subject to the jurisdiction thereof, are citizens of the United States and of the State wherein they reside. No State shall make or enforce any law which shall abridge the privileges or immunities of citizens of the United States; nor shall any State deprive any person of life, liberty, or property, without due process of law; nor deny to any person within its jurisdiction the equal protection of the laws.

Section 2. Representatives shall be apportioned among the several States according to their respective numbers, counting the whole number of persons in each State, excluding Indians not taxed. But when the right to vote at any election for the choice of electors for President and Vice President of the United States, Representatives in Congress, the Executive and Judicial officers of a State, or the members of the Legislature thereof, is denied to any of the male inhabitants of such State, being twenty-one years of age,[12] and citizens of the United States, or in any way abridged, except for participation in rebellion, or other crime, the basis of representation therein shall be reduced in the proportion which the number of such male citizens shall bear to the whole number of male citizens twenty-one years of age in such State.

Section 3. No person shall be a Senator or Representative in Congress, or elector of President and Vice President, or hold any office, civil or military, under the United States, or under any State, who, having previously taken an oath, as a member of Congress, or as an officer of the United States, or as a member of any State legislature, or as an executive or judicial officer of any State, to support the Constitution of the United States, shall have engaged in insurrection or rebellion against the same, or given aid or comfort to the enemies thereof. But Congress may by a vote of two-thirds of each House, remove such disability.

Section 4. The validity of the public debt of the United States, authorized by law, including debts incurred for payment of pensions and bounties for services in suppressing insurrection or rebellion, shall not be questioned. But neither the United States nor any State shall assume or pay any debt or obligation incurred in aid of insurrection or rebellion against the United States, or any claim for the loss or emancipation of any slave; but all such debts, obligations and claims shall be held illegal and void.

Section 5. The Congress shall have power to enforce, by appropriate legislation, the provisions of this article.

Amendment XV [Ratified February 3, 1870]

Section 1. The right of citizens of the United States to vote shall not be denied or abridged by the United States or by any State on account of race, color, or previous condition of servitude.

Section 2. The Congress shall have power to enforce this article by appropriate legislation.

Amendment XVI [Ratified February 3, 1913]

The Congress shall have power to lay and collect taxes on incomes, from whatever source derived, without apportionment among the several States, and without regard to any census or enumeration.

Amendment XVII [Ratified April 8, 1913]

The Senate of the United States shall be composed of two Senators from each State, elected by the people thereof, for six years; and each Senator shall have one vote. The electors in each State shall have the qualifications requisite for electors of the most numerous branch of the State legislatures.

When vacancies happen in the representation of any State in the Senate, the executive authority of such State shall issue writs of election to fill such vacancies: *Provided,* That the legislature of any State may empower the executive thereof to make temporary appointments until the people fill the vacancies by election as the legislature may direct.

This amendment shall not be so construed as to affect the election or term of any Senator chosen before it becomes valid as part of the Constitution.

[Amendment XVIII [Ratified January 16, 1919]

Section 1. After one year from the ratification of this article the manufacture, sale, or transportation of intoxicating liquors within, the importation thereof into, or the exportation thereof from the United States and all territory subject to the jurisdiction thereof for beverage purposes is hereby prohibited.

Section 2. The Congress and the several States shall have concurrent power to enforce this article by appropriate legislation.

Section 3. This article shall be inoperative unless it shall have been ratified as an amendment to the Constitution by the legislatures of the several States, as provided in the Constitution, within seven years from the date of the submission hereof to the States by the Congress.][13]

Amendment XIX [Ratified August 18, 1920]

The right of citizens of the United States to vote shall not be denied or abridged by the United States or by any State on account of sex.

Congress shall have power to enforce this article by appropriate legislation.

Amendment XX [Ratified January 23, 1933]

Section 1. The terms of the President and Vice President shall end at noon on the 20th day of January, and the terms of Senators and Representatives at noon on the 3d day of January, of the years in which such terms would have ended if this article had not been ratified; and the terms of their successors shall then begin.

Section 2. The Congress shall assemble at least once in every year, and such meeting shall begin at noon on the 3d day of January, unless they shall by law appoint a different day.

Section 3.[14] If, at the time fixed for the beginning of the term of the President, the President elect shall have died, the Vice President elect shall become President. If a President shall not have been chosen before the time fixed for the beginning of his term, or if the President elect shall have failed to qualify, then the Vice President elect shall act as President until a President shall have qualified; and the Congress may by law provide for the case wherein neither a President elect nor a Vice President elect shall have qualified, declaring who shall then act as President, or the manner in which one who is to act shall be selected, and such person shall act accordingly until a President or Vice President shall have qualified.

Section 4. The Congress may by law provide for the case of the death of any of the persons from whom the House of Representatives may choose a President whenever the right of choice shall have devolved upon them, and for the case of the death of any of the persons from whom the Senate may choose a Vice President whenever the right of choice shall have devolved upon them.

Section 5. *Sections 1 and 2 shall take effect on the 15th day of October following the ratification of this article.*

Section 6. *This article shall be inoperative unless it shall have been ratified as an amendment to the Constitution by the legislatures of three-fourths of the several States within seven years from the date of its submission.*

Amendment XXI [Ratified December 5, 1933]

Section 1. The eighteenth article of amendment to the Constitution of the United States is hereby repealed.

Section 2. The transportation or importation into any State, Territory, or possession of the United States for delivery or use therein of intoxicating liquors, in violation of the laws thereof, is hereby prohibited.

Section 3. This article shall be inoperative unless it shall have been ratified as an amendment to the Constitution by conventions in the several States, as provided in the Constitution, within seven years from the date of the submission hereof to the States by the Congress.

Amendment XXII [Ratified February 27, 1951]

Section 1. No person shall be elected to the office of the President more than twice, and no person who has held the office of President, or acted as President, for more than two years of a term to which some other person was elected President shall be elected to the office of the President more than once. But this Article shall not apply to any person holding the office of President when this Article was proposed by the Congress, and shall not prevent any person who may be holding the office of President, or acting as President, during the term within which this Article become operative from holding the office of President or acting as President during the remainder of such term.

Section 2. This article shall be inoperative unless it shall have been ratified as an amendment to the Constitution by the legislatures of three-fourths of the several States within seven years from the date of its submission to the States by the Congress.

Amendment XXIII [Ratified March 29, 1961]

Section 1. The District constituting the seat of Government of the United States shall appoint in such manner as the Congress may direct:

A number of electors of President and Vice President equal to the whole number of Senators and Representatives in Congress to which the District would be entitled if it were a State, but in no event more than the least populous State; they shall be in addition to those appointed by the States, but they shall be considered, for the purposes of the election of President and Vice President, to be electors appointed by a State; and they shall meet in the District and perform such duties as provided by the twelfth article of amendment.

Section 2. The Congress shall have power to enforce this article by appropriate legislation.

Amendment XXIV [Ratified January 23, 1964]

Section 1. The right of citizens of the United States to vote in any primary or other election for President or Vice President, for electors for President or Vice President, or for Senator or Representative in Congress, shall not be denied or abridged by the United States or any State by reason of failure to pay any poll tax or other tax.

Section 2. The Congress shall have power to enforce this article by appropriate legislation.

Amendment XXV [Ratified February 10, 1967]

Section 1. In case of the removal of the President from office or of his death or resignation, the Vice President shall become President.

Section 2. Whenever there is a vacancy in the office of the Vice President, the President shall nominate a Vice President who shall take office upon confirmation by a majority vote of both Houses of Congress.

Section 3. Whenever the President transmits to the President pro tempore of the Senate and the Speaker of the House of Representatives his written declaration that he is unable to discharge the powers and duties of his office, and until he transmits to them a written declaration to the contrary, such powers and duties shall be discharged by the Vice President as Acting President.

Section 4. Whenever the Vice President and a majority of either the principal officers of the executive departments or of such other body as Congress may by law provide, transmit to the President pro tempore of the Senate and the Speaker of the House of Representatives their written declaration that the President is unable to discharge the powers and duties of his office, the Vice President shall immediately assume the powers and duties of the office as Acting President.

Thereafter, when the President transmits to the President pro tempore of the Senate and the Speaker of the House of Representatives his written declaration that no inability exists, he shall resume the powers and duties of his office unless the Vice President and a majority of either the principal officers of the executive department or of such other body as Congress may by law provide, transmit within four days to the President pro tempore of the Senate and the Speaker of the House of Representatives their written declaration that the President is unable to discharge the powers and duties of his office. Thereupon Congress shall decide the issue, assembling within forty-eight hours for that purpose if not in session. If the Congress, within twenty-one days after receipt of the latter written declaration, or, if Congress is not in session, within twenty-one days after Congress is required to assemble, determines by two-thirds vote of both Houses that the President is unable to discharge the powers and duties of his office, the Vice President shall continue to discharge the same as Acting President; otherwise, the President shall resume the powers and duties of his office.

Amendment XXVI [Ratified July 1, 1971]

Section 1. The right of citizens of the United States, who are eighteen years of age or older, to vote shall not be denied or abridged by the United States or by any State on account of age.

Section 2. The Congress shall have power to enforce this article by appropriate legislation.

Amendment XXVII [Ratified May 7, 1992]

No law varying the compensation for the services of the Senators and Representatives shall take effect, until an election of Representatives shall have intervened.

NOTES

1. The part in brackets was changed by section 2 of the Fourteenth Amendment.
2. The part in brackets was changed by the first paragraph of the Seventeenth Amendment.
3. The part in brackets was changed by the second paragraph of the Seventeenth Amendment.
4. The part in brackets was changed by section 2 of the Twentieth Amendment.
5. The Sixteenth Amendment gave Congress the power to tax incomes.
6. The material in brackets has been superseded by the Twelfth Amendment.
7. This provision has been affected by the Twenty-fifth Amendment.
8. These clauses were affected by the Eleventh Amendment.
9. This paragraph has been superseded by the Thirteenth Amendment.
10. Obsolete.
11. The part in brackets has been superseded by section 3 of the Twentieth Amendment.
12. See the Nineteenth and Twenty-sixth Amendments.
13. This Amendment was repealed by section 1 of the Twenty-first Amendment.
14. See the Twenty-fifth Amendment.

Provisions of the U.S. Code

Title 3, United States Code—The President

Chapter 1. Presidential Elections and Vacancies

§ 1. Time of appointing electors
The electors of President and Vice President shall be appointed, in each State, on the Tuesday next after the first Monday in November, in every fourth year succeeding every election of a President and Vice President.

§ 2. Failure to make choice on prescribed day
Whenever any State has held an election for the purpose of choosing electors, and has failed to make a choice on the day prescribed by law, the electors may be appointed on a subsequent day in such a manner as the legislature of such State may direct.

§ 3. Number of electors
The number of electors shall be equal to the number of Senators and Representatives to which the several States are by law entitled at the time when the President and Vice President to be chosen come into office; except, that where no apportionment of Representatives has been made after any enumeration, at the time of choosing electors, the number of electors shall be according to the then existing apportionment of Senators and Representatives.

§ 4. Vacancies in electoral college
Each State may, by law, provide for the filling of any vacancies which may occur in its college of electors when such college meets to give its electoral vote.

§ 5. Determination of controversy as to appointment of electors
If any State shall have provided, by laws enacted prior to the day fixed for the appointment of the electors, for its final determination of any controversy or contest concerning the appointment of all or any of the electors of such State, by judicial or other methods or procedures, and such determination shall have been made at least six days before the time fixed for the meeting of the electors, such determination made pursuant to such law so existing on said day, and made at least six days prior to said time of meeting of the electors, shall be conclusive, and shall govern in the counting of the electoral votes as provided in the Constitution, and as hereinafter regulated, so far as the ascertainment of the electors appointed by such State is concerned.

§ 6. Credentials of electors; transmission to Archivist of the United States and to Congress; public inspection
It shall be the duty of the executive of each State, as soon as practicable after the conclusion of the appointment of the electors in such State by the final ascertainment, under and in pursuance of the laws of such State providing for such ascertainment, to communicate by registered mail under the seal of the State to the Archivist of the United States a certificate of such ascertainment of the electors appointed, setting forth the names of such electors and the canvass or other ascertainment under the laws of such State of the number of votes given or cast for each person for whose appointment any and all votes have been given or cast; and it shall also thereupon be the duty of the executive of each State to deliver to the electors of such State, on or before the day on which they are required by section 7 of this title [3 USC § 7] to meet, six duplicate-originals of the same certificate under the seal of the State; and if there shall have been any final determination in a State in the manner provided for by law of a controversy or contest concerning the appointment of all or any of the electors of such State, it shall be the duty of the executive of such State, as soon as practicable after such determination, to communicate under the seal of the State to the Archivist of the United States a certificate of such determination in form and manner as the same shall have been made; and the certificate or certificates so received by the Archivist of the United States shall be preserved by him for one year and shall be a part of the public records of his office and shall be open to public inspection; and the Archivist of the

United States at the first meeting of Congress thereafter shall transmit to the two Houses of Congress copies in full of each and every such certificate so received at the National Archives and Records Administration.

§ 7. Meeting and vote of electors

The electors of President and Vice President of each State shall meet and give their votes on the first Monday after the second Wednesday in December next following their appointment at such place in each State as the legislature of such State shall direct.

§ 8. Manner of voting

The electors shall vote for President and Vice President, respectively, in the manner directed by the Constitution.

§ 9. Certificates of votes for President and Vice President

The electors shall make and sign six certificates of all the votes given by them, each of which certificates shall contain two distinct lists, one of the votes for President and the other of the votes for Vice President, and shall annex to each of the certificates one of the lists of the electors which shall have been furnished to them by direction of the executive of the State.

§ 10. Sealing and endorsing certificates

The electors shall seal up the certificates so made by them, and certify upon each that the lists of all the votes of such State given for President, and of all the votes given for Vice President, are contained therein.

§ 11. Disposition of certificates

The electors shall dispose of the certificates so made by them and the lists attached thereto in the following manner: First. They shall forthwith forward by registered mail one of the same to the President of the Senate at the seat of government. Second. Two of the same shall be delivered to the secretary of state of the State, one of which shall be held subject to the order of the President of the Senate, the other to be preserved by him for one year and shall be a part of the public records of his office and shall be open to public inspection. Third. On the day thereafter they shall forward by registered mail two of such certificates and lists to the Archivist of the United States at the seat of government, one of which shall be held subject to the order of the President of the Senate. The other shall be preserved by the Archivist of the United States for one year and shall be a part of the public records of his office and shall be open to public inspection. Fourth. They shall forthwith cause the other of the certificates and lists to be delivered to the judge of the district in which the electors shall have assembled.

§ 12. Failure of certificates of electors to reach President of the Senate or Archivist of the United States; demand on State for certificate

When no certificate of vote and list mentioned in sections 9 and 11 of this title [3 USC §§ 9, 11] from any State shall have been received by the President of the Senate or by the Archivist of the United States by the fourth Wednesday in December, after the meeting of the electors shall have been held, the President of the Senate or, if he be absent from the seat of government, the Archivist of the United States shall request, by the most expeditious method available, the secretary of state of the State to send up the certificate and list lodged with him by the electors of such State; and it shall be his duty upon receipt of such request immediately to transmit same by registered mail to the President of the Senate at the seat of government.

§ 13. Same; demand on district judge for certificate

When no certificates of votes from any State shall have been received at the seat of government on the fourth Wednesday in December, after the meeting of the electors shall have been held, the President of the Senate or, if he be absent from the seat of government, the Archivist of the United States shall send a special messenger to the district judge in whose custody one certificate of votes from that State has been lodged, and such judge shall forthwith transmit that list by the hand of such messenger to the seat of government.

§ 14. Forfeiture for messenger's neglect of duty

Every person who, having been appointed, pursuant to section 13 of this title [3 USC § 13], to deliver the certificates of the votes of the electors to the President of the Senate, and having accepted such appointment, shall neglect to perform the services required from him, shall forfeit the sum of $1,000.

§ 15. Counting electoral votes in Congress

Congress shall be in session on the sixth day of January succeeding every meeting of the electors. The Senate and House of Representatives shall meet in the Hall of the House of Representatives at the hour of 1 o'clock in the afternoon on that day, and the President of the Senate shall be their presiding officer.

Two tellers shall be previously appointed on the part of the Senate and two on the part of the House of Representatives, to whom shall be handed, as they are opened by the President of the Senate, all the certificates and papers purporting to be certificates of the electoral votes, which certificates and papers shall be opened, presented, and acted upon in the alphabetical order of the States, beginning with the letter A; and said tellers, having then read the same in the presence and hearing of the two Houses, shall make a list of the votes as they shall appear from the said certificates; and the votes having been ascertained and counted according to the rules in this subchapter provided, the result of the same shall be delivered to the President of the Senate, who shall thereupon announce the state of the vote, which announcement shall be deemed a sufficient declaration of the persons, if any, elected President and Vice President of the United States, and, together with a list of the votes, be entered on the Journals of the two Houses.

Upon such reading of any such certificate or paper, the President of the Senate shall call for objections, if any. Every objection shall be made in writing, and shall state clearly and concisely, and without argument, the ground thereof, and shall be signed by at least one Senator and one Member of the House of Representatives before the same shall be received. When all objections so made to any vote or paper from a State shall have been received and read, the Senate shall thereupon withdraw, and such objections shall be submitted to the Senate for its decision; and the Speaker of the House of Representatives shall, in like manner, submit such objections to the House of Representatives for its decision; and no electoral vote or votes from any State which shall have been regularly given by electors whose appointment has been lawfully certified to according to section 6 of this title [3 USC § 6] from which but one return has been received shall be rejected, but the two Houses concurrently may reject the vote or votes when they agree that such vote or votes have not been so regularly given by electors whose appointment has been so certified.

If more than one return or paper purporting to be a return from a State shall have been received by the President of the Senate, those votes, and those only, shall be counted which shall have been regularly given by the electors who are shown by the determination mentioned in section 5 of this title [3 USC § 5] to have been appointed, if the determination in said section provided for shall have been made, or by such successors or substitutes, in case of a vacancy in the board of electors so ascertained, as have been appointed to fill such vacancy in the mode provided by the laws of the State; but in case there shall arise the question which of two or more of such State authorities determining what electors have been appointed, as mentioned in section 5 of this title [3 USC § 5], is the lawful tribunal of such State, the votes regularly given of those electors, and those only, of such State shall be counted whose title as electors the two Houses, acting separately, shall concurrently decide is supported by the decision of such State so authorized by its law; and in such case of more than one return or paper purporting to be a return from a State, if there shall have been no such determination of the question in the State aforesaid, then those votes, and those only, shall be counted which the two Houses shall concurrently decide were cast by lawful electors appointed in accordance with the laws of the State, unless the two Houses, acting separately, shall concurrently decide such votes not to be the lawful votes of the legally appointed electors of such State.

But if the two Houses shall disagree in respect of the counting of such votes, then, and in that case, the votes of the electors whose appointment shall have been certified by the executive of the State, under the seal thereof, shall be counted. When the two Houses have voted, they shall immediately again meet, and the presiding officer shall then announce the decision of the questions submitted. No votes or papers from any other State shall be acted upon until the objections previously made to the votes or papers from any State shall have been finally disposed of.

§ 16. Same; seats for officers and Members of two Houses in joint meeting

At such joint meeting of the two Houses seats shall be provided as follows: For the President of the Senate, the Speaker's chair; for the Speaker, immediately upon his left; the Senators, in the body of the Hall upon the right of the presiding officer; for the Representatives, in the body of the Hall not provided for the Senators; for the tellers, Secretary of the Senate, and Clerk of the House of Representatives, at the Clerk's desk; for the other officers of the two Houses, in front of the Clerk's desk and upon each side of the Speaker's platform. Such joint meeting shall not be dissolved until the count of electoral votes shall be completed and the result declared; and no recess shall be taken unless a question shall have arisen in regard to counting any such votes, or otherwise under this subchapter, in which case it shall be competent for either House, acting separately, in the manner hereinbefore provided, to direct a recess of such House not beyond the next calendar day, Sunday excepted, at the hour of 10 o'clock in the forenoon. But if the counting of the electoral votes and the declaration of the result shall not have been completed before the fifth calendar day next after such first meeting of the two Houses, no further or other recess shall be taken by either House.

§ 17. Same; limit of debate in each House
When the two Houses separate to decide upon an objection that may have been made to the counting of any electoral vote or votes from any State, or other question arising in the matter, each Senator and Representative may speak to such objection or question five minutes, and not more than once; but after such debate shall have lasted two hours it shall be the duty of the presiding officer of each House to put the main question without further debate.

§ 18. Same; parliamentary procedure at joint meeting
While the two Houses shall be in meeting as provided in this chapter [3 USC §§ 1 et seq.], the President of the Senate shall have power to preserve order; and no debate shall be allowed and no question shall be put by the presiding officer except to either House on a motion to withdraw.

§ 19. Vacancy in offices of both President and Vice President; officers eligible to act
(a)(1) If, by reason of death, resignation, removal from office, inability, or failure to qualify, there is neither a President nor Vice President to discharge the powers and duties of the office of President, then the Speaker of the House of Representatives shall, upon his resignation as Speaker and as Representative in Congress, act as President.

(2) The same rule shall apply in the case of the death, resignation, removal from office, or inability of an individual acting as President under this subsection.

(b) If, at the time when under subsection (a) of this section a Speaker is to begin the discharge of the powers and duties of the office of President, there is no Speaker, or the Speaker fails to qualify as Acting President, then the President pro tempore of the Senate shall, upon his resignation as President pro tempore and as Senator, act as President.

(c) An individual acting as President under subsection (a) or subsection (b) of this section shall continue to act until the expiration of the then-current Presidential term, except that

(1) if his discharge of the powers and duties of the office is founded in whole or in part on the failure of both the President-elect and the Vice-President-elect to qualify, then he shall act only until a President or Vice President qualifies; and

(2) if his discharge of the powers and duties of the office is founded in whole or in part on the inability of the President or Vice President, then he shall act only until the removal of the disability of one of such individuals.

(d)(1) If, by reason of death, resignation, removal from office, inability, or failure to qualify, there is no President pro tempore to act as President under subsection (b) of this section, then the officer of the United States who is highest on the following list, and who is not under disability to discharge the powers and duties of the office of President shall act as President: Secretary of State, Secretary of the Treasury, Secretary of Defense, Attorney General, Secretary of the Interior, Secretary of Agriculture, Secretary of Commerce, Secretary of Labor, Secretary of Health and Human Services, Secretary of Housing and Urban Development, Secretary of Transportation, Secretary of Energy, Secretary of Education, Secretary of Veterans Affairs.

(2) An individual acting as President under this subsection shall continue so to do until the expiration of the then current Presidential term, but not after a qualified and prior-entitled individual is able to act, except that the removal of the disability of an individual higher on the list contained in paragraph (1) of this subsection or the ability to qualify on the part of an individual higher on such list shall not terminate his service.

(3) The taking of the oath of office by an individual specified in the list in paragraph (1) of this subsection shall be held to constitute his resignation from the office by virtue of the holding of which he qualifies to act as President.

(e) Subsections (a), (b), and (d) of this section shall apply only to such officers as are eligible to the office of President under the Constitution. Subsection (d) of this section shall apply only to officers appointed, by and with the advice and consent of the Senate, prior to the time of the death, resignation, removal from office, inability, or failure to qualify, of the President pro tempore, and only to officers not under impeachment by the House of Representatives at the time the powers and duties of the office of President devolve upon them.

(f) During the period that any individual acts as President under this section, his compensation shall be at the rate then provided by law in the case of the President.

§ 20. Resignation or refusal of office

The only evidence of a refusal to accept, or of a resignation of the office of President or Vice President, shall be an instrument in writing, declaring the same, and subscribed by the person refusing to accept or resigning, as the case may be, and delivered into the office of the Secretary of State.

§ 21. Definitions

As used in this chapter [3 USC §§ 1 et seq.] the term

(a) "State" includes the District of Columbia.

(b) "executives of each State" includes the Board of Commissioners of the District of Columbia.

Appendix C

Supreme Court Cases

WILLIAMS ET AL. V. RHODES, GOVERNOR OF OHIO, ET AL. 393 U.S. 23 (1968)

MR. JUSTICE BLACK delivered the opinion of the Court.

The State of Ohio in a series of election laws has made it virtually impossible for a new political party, even though it has hundreds of thousands of members, or an old party, which has a very small number of members, to be placed on the state ballot to choose electors pledged to particular candidates for the Presidency and Vice Presidency of the United States.

Ohio Revised Code, § 3517.01, requires a new party to obtain petitions signed by qualified electors totaling 15% of the number of ballots cast in the last preceding gubernatorial election. The detailed provisions of other Ohio election laws result in the imposition of substantial additional burdens, which were accurately summarized in Judge Kinneary's dissenting opinion in the court below and were substantially agreed on by the other members of that court. Together these various restrictive provisions make it virtually impossible for any party to qualify on the ballot except the Republican and Democratic Parties. These two Parties face substantially smaller burdens because they are allowed to retain their positions on the ballot simply by obtaining 10% of the votes in the last gubernatorial election and need not obtain any signature petitions. Moreover, Ohio laws make no provision for ballot position for independent candidates as distinguished from political parties.

* * *

I.

Ohio's claim that the political-question doctrine precludes judicial consideration of these cases requires very little discussion. That claim has been rejected in cases of this kind numerous times. It was rejected by the Court unanimously in 1892 in the case of McPherson v. Blacker, 146 U.S. 1, 23-24, and more recently it has been squarely rejected in Baker v. Carr, 369 U.S. 186, 208-237 (1962), and in Wesberry v. Sanders, 376 U.S. 1, 5-7 (1964). Other cases to the same effect need not now be cited. These cases do raise a justiciable controversy under the Constitution and cannot be relegated to the political arena.

II.

The State also contends that it has absolute power to put any burdens it pleases on the selection of electors because of the First Section of the Second Article of the Constitution, providing that "Each State shall appoint, in such Manner as the Legislature thereof may direct, a Number of Electors . . ." to choose a President and Vice President. There, of course, can be no question but that this section does grant extensive power to the States to pass laws regulating the selection of electors. But the Constitution is filled with provisions that grant Congress or the States specific power to legislate in certain areas; these granted powers are always subject to the limitation that they may not be exercised in a way that violates other specific provisions of the Constitution. For example, Congress is granted broad power to "lay and collect Taxes," but the taxing power, broad as it is, may not be invoked in such a way as to violate the privilege against self-incrimination. Nor can it be thought that the power to select electors could be exercised in such a way as to violate express constitutional commands that specifically bar States from passing certain kinds of laws. Clearly, the Fifteenth and Nineteenth Amendments were intended to bar the Federal Government and the States from denying the right to vote on grounds of race and sex in presidential elections. And the Twenty-fourth Amendment clearly and literally bars any State from imposing a poll tax on the right to vote "for electors for President or Vice President." Obviously we must reject the notion that Art. II, § 1, gives the States power to impose burdens on the right to vote, where such burdens are expressly prohibited in other constitutional provisions. We therefore hold that no State can pass a law regulating elections that violates the Fourteenth Amendment's command that "No State shall . . . deny to any person . . . the equal protection of the laws."

III.

We turn then to the question whether the court below properly held that the Ohio laws before us result in a denial of equal protection of the laws. It is true that this Court has firmly established the principle that the Equal Protection Clause does not make every minor difference in the application of laws to different groups a violation of our Constitution. But we have also held many times that "invidious" distinctions cannot be enacted without a violation of the Equal Protection Clause. In determining whether or not a state law violates the Equal Protection Clause, we must consider the facts and circumstances behind the law, the interests which the State claims to be protecting, and the interests of those who are disadvantaged by the classification. In the present situation the state laws place burdens on two different, although overlapping, kinds of rights—the right of individuals to associate for the advancement of political beliefs, and the right of qualified voters, regardless of their political persuasion, to cast their votes effectively. Both of these rights, of course, rank among our most precious freedoms. We have repeatedly held that freedom of association is protected by the First Amendment. And of course this freedom protected against federal encroachment by the First Amendment is entitled under the Fourteenth Amendment to the same protection from infringement by the States. Similarly we have said with reference to the right to vote: "No right is more precious in a free country than that of having a voice in the election of those who make the laws under which, as good citizens, we must live. Other rights, even the most basic, are illusory if the right to vote is undermined."

No extended discussion is required to establish that the Ohio laws before us give the two old, established parties a decided advantage over any new parties struggling for existence and thus place substantially unequal burdens on both the right to vote and the right to associate. The right to form a party for the advancement of political goals means little if a party can be kept off the election ballot and thus denied an equal opportunity to win votes. So also, the right to vote is heavily burdened if that vote may be cast only for one of two parties at a time when other parties are clamoring for a place on the ballot. In determining whether the State has power to place such unequal burdens on minority groups where rights of this kind are at stake, the decisions of this Court have consistently held that "only a compelling state interest in the regulation of a subject within the State's constitutional power to regulate can justify limiting First Amendment freedoms." NAACP v. Button, 371 U.S. 415, 438 (1963).

The State has here failed to show any "compelling interest" which justifies imposing such heavy burdens on the right to vote and to associate.

The State asserts that the following interests are served by the restrictions it imposes. It claims that the State may validly promote a two-party system in order to encourage compromise and political stability. The fact is, however, that the Ohio system does not merely favor a "two-party system"; it favors two particular parties—the Republicans and the Democrats—and in effect tends to give them a complete monopoly. There is, of course, no reason why two parties should retain a permanent monopoly on the right to have people vote for or against them. Competition in ideas and governmental policies is at the core of our electoral process and of the First Amendment freedoms. New parties struggling for their place must have the time and opportunity to organize in order to meet reasonable requirements for ballot position, just as the old parties have had in the past.

Ohio makes a variety of other arguments to support its very restrictive election laws. It points out, for example, that if three or more parties are on the ballot, it is possible that no one party would obtain 50% of the vote, and the runner-up might have been preferred to the plurality winner by a majority of the voters. Concededly, the State does have an interest in attempting to see that the election winner be the choice of a majority of its voters. But to grant the State power to keep all political parties off the ballot until they have enough members to win would stifle the growth of all new parties working to increase their strength from year to year. Considering these Ohio laws in their totality, this interest cannot justify the very severe restrictions on voting and associational rights which Ohio has imposed.

The State also argues that its requirement of a party structure and an organized primary insures that those who disagree with the major parties and their policies "will be given a choice of leadership as well as issues" since any leader who attempts to capitalize on the disaffection of such a group is forced to submit to a primary in which other, possibly more attractive, leaders can raise the same issues and compete for the allegiance of the disaffected group. But while this goal may be desirable, Ohio's system cannot achieve it. Since the principal policies of the major parties change to some extent from year to year, and since the identity of the likely major party nominees may not be known until shortly before the election, this disaffected "group" will rarely if ever be a cohesive or identifiable group until a few months before the election. Thus, Ohio's burdensome procedures, requiring extensive organization and other election activities by a very early date, operate to prevent such a group from ever getting on the ballot and the Ohio system thus denies the "disaffected" not only a choice of leadership but a choice on the issues as well.

Finally Ohio claims that its highly restrictive provisions are justified because without them a large number of parties might qualify for the ballot, and the voters would then be confronted with a choice so confusing that the popular will could be frustrated. But the experience of many States, including that of Ohio prior to 1948, demonstrates that no more than a handful of parties attempts to qualify for ballot positions even when a very low number of signatures, such as 1% of the electorate, is required.° It is true that the existence of multitudinous fragmentary groups might justify some regulatory control but in Ohio at the present time this danger seems to us no more than "theoretically imaginable." No such remote danger can justify the immediate and crippling impact on the basic constitutional rights involved in this case.

Of course, the number of voters in favor of a party, along with other circumstances, is relevant in considering whether state laws violate the Equal Protection Clause. And, as we have said, the State is left with broad powers to regulate voting, which may include laws relating to the qualification and functions of electors. But here the totality of the Ohio restrictive laws taken as a whole imposes a burden on voting and associational rights which we hold is an invidious discrimination, in violation of the Equal Protection Clause.

* * *

MR. JUSTICE DOUGLAS.

* * *

The selection of presidential electors is provided in Art. II, § 1, of the Constitution. It is unnecessary in this case to decide whether electors are state rather than federal officials, whether States may select them through appointment rather than by popular vote, or whether there is a constitutional right to vote for them. For in this

---

° Forty-two States require third parties to obtain the signatures of only 1% or less of the electorate in order to appear on the ballot. It appears that no significant problem has arisen in these States which have relatively lenient requirements for obtaining ballot position.

case Ohio has already provided for them to be chosen by right of popular suffrage. Having done so, the question is whether Ohio may encumber that right with conditions of the character imposed here.

* * *

The First Amendment, made applicable to the States by reason of the Fourteenth Amendment, lies at the root of these cases. The right of association is one form of "orderly group activity" (NAACP v. Button, 371 U.S. 415, 430), protected by the First Amendment. The right "to engage in association for the advancement of beliefs and ideas" (NAACP v. Alabama, 357 U.S. 449, 460), is one activity of that nature that has First Amendment protection. As we said in Bates v. Little Rock, 361 U.S. 516, 523, "freedom of association for the purpose of advancing ideas and airing grievances is protected by the Due Process Clause of the Fourteenth Amendment from invasion by the States." And see Louisiana v. NAACP, 366 U.S. 293, 296. At the root of the present controversy is the right to vote— a "fundamental political right" that is "preservative of all rights." Yick Wo v. Hopkins, 118 U.S. 356, 370. The rights of expression and assembly may be "illusory if the right to vote is undermined." Wesberry v. Sanders, 376 U.S. 1, 17.

In our political life, third parties are often important channels through which political dissent is aired: "All political ideas cannot and should not be channeled into the programs of our two major parties. History has amply proved the virtue of political activity by minority, dissident groups, which innumerable times have been in the vanguard of democratic thought and whose programs were ultimately accepted.... The absence of such voices would be a symptom of grave illness in our society." Sweezy v. New Hampshire, 354 U.S. 234, 250-251 (opinion of WARREN, C. J.).

The Equal Protection Clause of the Fourteenth Amendment permits the States to make classifications and does not require them to treat different groups uniformly. Nevertheless, it bans any "invidious discrimination." Harper v. Virginia Board of Elections, 383 U.S. 663, 667.

That command protects voting rights and political groups (Carrington v. Rash, 380 U.S. 89), as well as economic units, racial communities, and other entities. When "fundamental rights and liberties" are at issue (Harper v. Virginia Board, supra, at 670), a State has less leeway in making classifications than when it deals with economic matters. I would think that a State has precious little leeway in making it difficult or impossible for citizens to vote for whomsoever they please and to organize campaigns for any school of thought they may choose, whatever part of the spectrum it reflects.

Cumbersome election machinery can effectively suffocate the right of association, the promotion of political ideas and programs of political action, and the right to vote. The totality of Ohio's requirements has those effects. It is unnecessary to decide whether Ohio has an interest, "compelling" or not, in abridging those rights, because "the men who drafted our Bill of Rights did all the 'balancing' that was to be done in this field." Konigsberg v. State Bar, 366 U.S. 36, 61 (BLACK, J., dissenting). Appellees would imply that "no kind of speech is to be protected if the Government can assert an interest of sufficient weight to induce this Court to uphold its abridgment." (Id., at 67.) I reject that suggestion.

* * *

MR. JUSTICE HARLAN, concurring in the result.

I agree that the American Independent Party is entitled to have the names of its Presidential and Vice Presidential candidates placed on the Ohio ballot in the forthcoming election, but that, for the practical reasons stated by the Court, the Socialist Labor Party is not. However, I would rest this decision entirely on the proposition that Ohio's statutory scheme violates the basic right of political association assured by the First Amendment which is protected against state infringement under the Due Process Clause of the Fourteenth Amendment. It is true that Ohio has not directly limited appellants' right to assemble or discuss public issues or solicit new members. Instead, by denying the appellants any opportunity to participate in the procedure by which the President is selected, the State has eliminated the basic incentive that all political parties have for conducting such activities, thereby depriving appellants of much of the substance, if not the form, of their protected rights. The right to have one's voice heard and one's views considered by the appropriate governmental authority is at the core of the right of political association.

It follows that the particular method by which Presidential Electors are chosen is not of decisive importance to a solution of the constitutional problem before us. Just as a political group has a right to organize effectively so that its position may be heard in court, so it has the right to place its candidate for the Presidency before whatever body has the power to make the State's selection of Electors. Consequently, it makes no difference that the State of Ohio may, under the Second Article of the Constitution, place the power of Electoral selection beyond the control of the general electorate. The requirement imposed by the Due Process Clause remains the same—no matter what the institution to which the decision is entrusted, political groups have a right to be heard before it. A statute that would require that all Electors be members of the two major parties is subject to the same constitutional challenge regardless of whether it is the legislature, the people, or some other body that is empowered to make the ultimate decision under the laws of the State.

Of course, the State may limit the right of political association by invoking an impelling policy justification for doing so. But as my Brother BLACK's opinion demonstrates, Ohio has been able to advance no such justification for denying almost half a million of its citizens their fundamental right to organize effectively for political purposes. Consequently, it may not exclude them from the process by which Presidential Electors are selected.

In deciding this case of first impression, I think it unnecessary to draw upon the Equal Protection Clause. I am by no means clear that equal protection doctrine, especially as it has been propounded in the recent state reapportionment cases, e. g., Reynolds v. Sims, 377 U.S. 533 (1964), may properly be applied to adjudicate disputes involving the mere procedure by which the President is selected, as that process is governed by profoundly different principles.[2] Despite my doubts on this score, I think it perfectly consistent and appropriate to hold the Due Process Clause applicable. For I believe that our task is more difficult than one which involves merely the mechanical application of the commands to be found in the Fourteenth Amendment or in the first section of the Second Article to the Constitution. Rather, we must attempt to accommodate as best we may the narrow provision drafted by the Philadelphia Convention with the broad principles announced in the Fourteenth Amendment, generations later.

---

[2] At no stage in the complex process by which a President is chosen is the "one man, one vote" principle of Reynolds v. Sims followed. The constitutional decision to grant each State at least three Electors, regardless of population, was a necessary part of the effort to gain the consent of the small States, as was the provision that when the choice of the President fell to the House, each state delegation would cast but one vote.

A decision resting solely upon the Due Process Clause would permit such an accommodation—for such a holding fully respects the original purposes and early development of the Electoral College. When one looks beyond the language of Article II, and considers the Convention's understanding of the College, Ohio's restrictive approach is seen to undermine what the draftsmen understood to be its very essence. The College was created to permit the most knowledgeable members of the community to choose the executive of a nation whose continental dimensions were thought to preclude an informed choice by the citizenry at large. If a State declares that an entire class of citizens is ineligible for the position of Elector, and that class is defined in a way in which individual merit plays no part, it strikes at the very basis of the College as it was originally conceived.

The constitutional grant of power to the States was intended for a different purpose. While Madison reports that the popular election of Electors on a district-by-district basis was the method "mostly, if not exclusively, in view when the Constitution was framed and adopted," 3 M. Farrand, The Records of the Federal Convention of 1787, p. 459 (1911), it is quite clear that a significant, if not dominant, group at the Convention contemplated that Electors would be chosen by other methods. It was to accommodate these members that the state legislatures were given their present leeway. While during the first four decades of the Republic, the States did in fact adopt a variety of methods for selecting their Electors, the parties in this case have pointed to, and I have found, no case in which the legislature attempted by statute to restrict the class of the enfranchised citizenry that could be considered for the office by whatever body was to make the choice.

Nothing in the history of the Electoral College from the moment of its inception, then, indicates that the original understanding of that institution would at all be compromised if we refuse to read the language of Art. II, § 1, as granting a power of arbitrary action which is so radically inconsistent with the general principles of the Due Process Clause. Consequently, there is no obstacle to a holding which denies the States, absent an overriding state interest, the right to prevent third parties from having an opportunity to put their candidates before the attention of the voters or whatever other body the State has designated as the one which is to choose Electors.

* * *

MR. JUSTICE STEWART, dissenting.

If it were the function of this Court to impose upon the States our own ideas of wise policy, I might be inclined to join my Brethren in compelling the Ohio election authorities to disregard the laws enacted by the legislature of that State. We deal, however, not with a question of policy, but with a problem of constitutional power. And to me it is clear that, under the Constitution as it is written, the Ohio Legislature has the power to do what it has done.

I.

The Constitution does not provide for popular election of a President or Vice President of the United States, either nationally or on a state-by-state basis. On the contrary, the Constitution explicitly specifies:

"Each State shall *appoint, in such Manner as the Legislature thereof may direct,* a Number of Electors, equal to the whole Number of Senators and Representatives to which the State may be entitled in the Congress...." (Emphasis supplied.)

"The Electors shall meet in their respective states and vote by ballot for President and Vice-President...."

Chief Justice Fuller, therefore, was stating no more than the obvious when he wrote for a unanimous Court in McPherson v. Blacker, 146 U.S. 1, more than 75 years ago:

"The Constitution does not provide that the appointment of electors shall be by popular vote, nor that the electors shall be voted for upon a general ticket, nor that the majority of those who exercise the elective franchise can alone choose the electors. It recognizes that the people act through their representatives in the legislature, and leaves it to the legislature exclusively to define the method of effecting the object....

"In short, the appointment and mode of appointment of electors belong exclusively to the States under the Constitution of the United States...." Id., at 27, 35.

A State is perfectly free under the Constitution to provide for the selection of its presidential electors by the legislature itself. Such a process of appointment was in fact utilized by several States throughout our early history, and by one State, Colorado, as late as 1876. Or a state legislature might nominate two slates of electors, and allow all eligible voters of the State to choose between them. Indeed, many of the States formerly provided for the appointment of presidential electors by various kinds of just such cooperative action of their legislatures and their electorates.

For a fuller description of the diverse methods pursued by the States in appointing their electors under Art. II, § 1, during this Country's first century of constitutional experience, see id., at 26-35.

Here, the Ohio Legislature has gone further, and has provided for a choice by the State's eligible voters among slates of electors put forward by all political parties that meet the even-handed requirements of long-standing state laws. We are told today, however, that, despite the power explicitly granted to the state legislatures under Art. II, § 1, the Legislature of Ohio nonetheless violated the Constitution in providing for the selection of electors in this way. I can perceive no such constitutional violation.

I agree with my Brethren that, in spite of the broad language of Art. II, § 1, a state legislature is not completely unfettered in choosing whatever process it may wish for the appointment of electors. Three separate constitutional amendments explicitly limit a legislature's power. The Fifteenth Amendment makes clear that if voters are to be included in the process, no voter may be excluded "on account of race, color, or previous condition of servitude." The Nineteenth Amendment makes equally clear that no voter may be excluded "on account of sex." And the Twenty-fourth Amendment prohibits exclusion of any voter "by reason of failure to pay any poll tax or other tax." But no claim has been or could be made in this case that any one of these Amendments has been violated by Ohio.

Rather, it is said that Ohio has violated the provisions of the Fourteenth Amendment. The Court holds that the State has violated that Clause of the Amendment which prohibits it from denying "to any person within its jurisdiction the equal protection of the laws." And two concurring opinions emphasize First Amendment principles, made applicable to the States through the Fourteenth Amendment's guarantees, in summarily concluding that Ohio's statutory scheme is invalid. I concede that the Fourteenth Amendment imposes some limitations upon a state legislature's freedom to choose a method for the appointment of electors. A State may not, for example, adopt a system that discriminates on grounds of religious or political belief. But I cannot agree that Ohio's system violates the Fourteenth Amendment in any way.

* * *

V.

It is thought by a great many people that the entire electoral college system of presidential selection set up by the Constitution is an anachronism in need of major overhaul. As a citizen, I happen to share that view. But this Court must follow the Constitution as it is written, and Art. II, § 1, vests in the States the broad discretion to select their presidential electors as they see fit. The method Ohio has chosen may be unwise as a matter of policy, but I cannot agree that it violates the Constitution.

MR. JUSTICE WHITE, dissented in part and concurred in part.

MR. CHIEF JUSTICE WARREN, dissented.

McPHERSON v. BLACKER
146 U.S. 1 (1892)

[The Michigan statute governing the appointment by district of presidential electors specified a date for their meeting that was different from the date set forth in federal legislation.]

MR. CHIEF JUSTICE FULLER, after stating the case as above reported, delivered the opinion of the court.

* * *

On behalf of plaintiffs in error it is contended that the act is void because in conflict with (1) clause two of section one of Article II of the Constitution of the United States; (2) the Fourteenth and Fifteenth Amendments to the Constitution; and (3) the act of Congress of February 3, 1887.

The second clause of section one of Article II of the Constitution is in these words: "Each State shall appoint, in such Manner as the Legislature thereof may direct, a Number of Electors, equal to the whole Number of Senators and Representatives to which the State may be entitled in the Congress; but no Senator or Representative, or Person holding an Office of Trust or Profit under the United States, shall be appointed an Elector."

The manner of the appointment of electors directed by the act of Michigan is the election of an elector and an alternate elector in each of the twelve Congressional districts into which the State of Michigan is divided, and of an elector and an alternate elector at large in each of two districts defined by the act. It is insisted that it was not competent for the legislature to direct this manner of appointment because the State is to appoint as a body politic and corporate, and so must act as a unit and cannot delegate the authority to subdivisions created for the purpose; and it is argued that the appointment of electors by districts is not an appointment by the State, because all its citizens otherwise qualified are not permitted to vote for all the presidential electors.

"A State in the ordinary sense of the Constitution," said Chief Justice Chase, Texas v. White, 7 Wall. 700, 721, "is a political community of free citizens, occupying a territory of defined boundaries, and organized under a government sanctioned and limited by a written constitution, and established by the consent of the governed." The State does not act by its people in their collective capacity, but through such political agencies as are duly constituted and established. The legislative power is the supreme authority except as limited by the constitution of the State, and the sovereignty of the people is exercised through their representatives in the legislature unless by the fundamental law power is elsewhere reposed. The Constitution of the United States frequently refers to the State as a political community, and also in terms to the people of the several States and the citizens of each State. What is forbidden or required to be done by a State is forbidden or required of the legislative power under state constitutions as they exist.

The clause under consideration does not read that the people or the citizens shall appoint, but that "each State shall"; and if the words "in such manner as the legislature thereof may direct," had been omitted, it would seem that the legislative power of appointment could not have been successfully questioned in the absence of any provision in the state constitution in that regard. Hence the insertion of those words, while operating as a limitation upon the State in respect of any attempt to circumscribe the legislative power, cannot be held to operate as a limitation on that power itself.

If the legislature possesses plenary authority to direct the manner of appointment, and might itself exercise the appointing power by joint ballot or concurrence of the two houses, or according to such mode as designated, it is difficult to perceive why, if the legislature prescribes as a method of appointment choice by vote, it must necessarily be by general ticket and not by districts. In other words, the act of appointment is none the less the act of the State in its entirety because arrived at by districts, for the act is the act of political agencies duly authorized to speak for the State, and the combined result is the expression of the voice of the State, a result reached by direction of the legislature, to whom the whole subject is committed.

By the first paragraph of section two, Article I, it is provided: "The House of Representatives shall be composed of Members chosen every second year by the people of the several States, and the Electors in each State shall have the Qualifications requisite for Electors of the most numerous Branch of the State Legislature"; and by the third paragraph "when vacancies happen in the Representation from any State, the Executive Authority thereof shall issue Writs of Election to fill such Vacancies." Section four reads: "The Times, Places and Manner of holding Elections for Senators and Representatives, shall be prescribed in each State by the Legislature thereof; but the Congress may at anytime by Law make or alter such Regulations, except as to the Places of choosing Senators."

Although it is thus declared that the people of the several States shall choose the members of Congress, (language which induced the State of New York to insert a salvo as to the power to divide into districts, in its resolutions of ratification,) the state legislatures, prior to 1842, in prescribing the times, places and manner of holding elections for representatives, had usually apportioned the State into districts, and assigned to each a representative; and by act of Congress of June 25, 1842, 5 Stat. 491, c. 47, (carried forward as § 23 of the Revised Statutes), it was provided that where a State was entitled to more than one representative, the election should be by districts. It has never been doubted that representatives in Congress thus chosen represented the entire people of the State acting in their sovereign capacity.

By original clause three of section one of Article II, and by the Twelfth Amendment which superseded that clause, in case of a failure in the election of President by the people, the House of Representatives is to choose the President; and "the vote shall be taken by States, the representation from each State having one vote." The State acts as a unit and its vote is given as a unit, but that vote is arrived at through the votes of its representatives in Congress elected by districts.

The State also acts individually through its electoral college, although, by reason of the power of its legislature over the manner of appointment, the vote of its electors may be divided.

The Constitution does not provide that the appointment of electors shall be by popular vote, nor that the electors shall be voted for upon a general ticket, nor that the majority of those who exercise the elective franchise can alone choose the electors. It recognizes that the people act through their representatives in the legislature, and leaves it to the legislature exclusively to define the method of effecting the object.

The framers of the Constitution employed words in their natural sense; and where they are plain and clear, resort to collateral aids to interpretation is unnecessary and cannot be indulged in to narrow or enlarge the text; but where there is ambiguity or doubt, or where two views may well be entertained, contemporaneous and subsequent practical construction are entitled to the greatest weight. Certainly, plaintiffs in error cannot reasonably assert that the clause of the Constitution under consideration so plainly sustains their position as to entitle them to object that contemporaneous history and practical construction are not to be allowed their legitimate force, and, conceding that their argument inspires a doubt sufficient to justify resort to the aids of interpretation thus afforded, we are of opinion that such doubt is thereby resolved against them, the contemporaneous practical exposition of the Constitution being too strong and obstinate to be shaken or controlled. Stuart v. Laird, 1 Cranch, 299, 309.

It has been said that the word "appoint" is not the most appropriate word to describe the result of a popular election. Perhaps not; but it is sufficiently comprehensive to cover that mode, and was manifestly used as conveying the broadest power of determination. It was used in Article V of the Articles of Confederation, which provided that "delegates shall be annually appointed in such manner as the legislature of each State shall direct"; and in the resolution of Congress of February 21, 1787, which declared it expedient that "a convention of delegates who shall have been appointed by the several States," should be held.

The appointment of delegates was, in fact, made by the legislatures directly, but that involved no denial of authority to direct some other mode. The Constitutional Convention, by resolution of September 17, 1787, expressed the opinion that the Congress should fix a day "on which electors should be appointed by the States which shall have ratified the same," etc., and that "after such publication, the electors should be appointed, and the Senators and Representatives elected."

The Journal of the Convention discloses that propositions that the President should be elected by "the citizens of the United States," or by the "people," or "by electors to be chosen by the people of the several States," instead of by the Congress, were voted down, (Jour.

Con. 286, 288; 1 Elliot's Deb. 208, 262,) as was the proposition that the President should be "chosen by electors appointed for that purpose by the legislatures of the States," though at one time adopted. Jour. Con. 190; 1 Elliot's Deb. 208, 211, 217. And a motion to postpone the consideration of the choice "by the national legislature," in order to take up a resolution providing for electors to be elected by the qualified voters in districts, was negatived in Committee of the Whole. Jour. Con. 92; 1 Elliot's Deb. 156. Gerry proposed that the choice should be made by the State executives; Hamilton, that the election be by electors chosen by electors chosen by the people; James Wilson and Gouverneur Morris were strongly in favor of popular vote; Ellsworth and Luther Martin preferred the choice by electors elected by the legislatures; and Roger Sherman, appointment by Congress. The final result seems to have reconciled contrariety of views by leaving it to the state legislatures to appoint directly by joint ballot or concurrent separate action, or through popular election by districts or by general ticket, or as otherwise might be directed.

Therefore, on reference to contemporaneous and subsequent action under the clause, we should expect to find, as we do, that various modes of choosing the electors were pursued, as, by the legislature itself on joint ballot; by the legislature through a concurrent vote of the two houses; by vote of the people for a general ticket; by vote of the people in districts; by choice partly by the people voting in districts and partly by the legislature; by choice by the legislature from candidates voted for by the people in districts; and in other ways, as, notably, by North Carolina in 1792, and Tennessee in 1796 and 1800. No question was raised as to the power of the State to appoint, in any mode its legislature saw fit to adopt, and none that a single method, applicable without exception, must be pursued in the absence of an amendment to the Constitution. The district system was largely considered the most equitable, and Madison wrote that it was that system which was contemplated by the framers of the Constitution, although it was soon seen that its adoption by some States might place them at a disadvantage by a division of their strength, and that a uniform rule was preferable.

At the first presidential election the appointment of electors was made by the legislatures of Connecticut, Delaware, Georgia, New Jersey and South Carolina. Pennsylvania, by act of October 4, 1788, Acts Penn. 1787-1788, p. 513, provided for the election of electors on a general ticket. Virginia, by act of November 17, 1788, was divided into twelve separate districts and an elector elected in each district, while for the election of Congressmen the State was divided into ten other districts. Laws Va. Oct. Sess. 1788, pp. 1, 2; 12 Henning's Stat. 648. In Massachusetts the general court, by resolve of November 17, 1788, divided the State into districts for the election of Representatives in Congress, and provided for their election December 18, 1788, and that at the same time the qualified inhabitants of each district should give their votes for two persons as candidates for an elector of President and Vice President of the United States, and, from the two persons in each district having the greatest number of votes, the two houses of the general court by joint ballot should elect one as elector, and in the same way should elect two electors at large. Mass. Resolves, 1788, p. 53. In Maryland, under act of December 22, 1788, electors were elected on general ticket, five being residents of the Western Shore and three of the Eastern Shore. Laws Md. 1788, Nov. Sess. c. 10. In New Hampshire an act was passed November 12, 1788, Laws N.H. 1789, p. 167, providing for the election of five electors by majority popular vote, and in case of no choice that the legislature should appoint out of so many of the candidates as equalled double the number of electors elected. There being no choice the appointment was made by the legislature. The senate would not agree to a joint ballot, and the house was compelled, that the vote of the State might not be lost, to concur in the electors chosen by the senate. The State of New York lost its vote through a similar contest. The assembly was willing to elect by joint ballot of the two branches or to divide the electors with the senate, but the senate would assent to nothing short of a complete negative upon the action of the assembly, and the time for election passed without an appointment. North Carolina and Rhode Island had not then ratified the Constitution.

Fifteen States participated in the second presidential election, in nine of which electors were chosen by the legislatures. Maryland, (Laws Md. 1790, c. 16, [2 Kelty]; Laws 1791, c. 62, [2 Kelty],) New Hampshire, (Laws N.H. 1792, 398, 401,) and Pennsylvania (Laws Penn. 1792, p. 240,) elected their electors on a general ticket, and Virginia by districts. Laws Va. 1792, p. 87, [13 Henning, 536]. In Massachusetts the general court by resolution of June 30, 1792, divided the State into four districts, in each of two of which five electors were elected, and in each of the other two three electors.

Mass. Resolves, June, 1792, p. 25. Under the apportionment of April 13, 1792, North Carolina was entitled to ten members of the House of Representatives. The legislature was not in session and did not meet until November 15, while under the act of Congress of March 1, 1792, (1 Stat. 239, c. 8,) the electors were to assemble on December 5. The legislature passed an act dividing the State into four districts, and directing the members of the legislature residing in each district to meet on the 25th of November and choose three electors. 2 Iredell N. Car. Laws, 1715 to 1800, c. 15 of 1792. At the same session an act was passed dividing the State into districts for the election of electors in 1796, and every four years thereafter. Id. c. 16.

Sixteen States took part in the third presidential election, Tennessee having been admitted June 1, 1796. In nine States the electors were appointed by the legislatures, and in Pennsylvania and New Hampshire by popular vote for a general ticket. Virginia, North Carolina, and Maryland elected by districts. The Maryland law of December 24, 1795, was entitled "An act to alter the mode of electing electors," and provided for dividing the State into ten districts, each of which districts should "elect and appoint one person, being a resident of the said district, as an elector." Laws Md. 1795, c. 73, [2 Kelty]. Massachusetts adhered to the district system, electing one elector in each Congressional district by a majority vote. It was provided that if no one had a majority, the legislature should make the appointment on joint ballot, and the legislature also appointed two electors at large in the same manner. Mass. Resolves, June, 1796, p. 12. In Tennessee an act was passed August 8, 1796, which provided for the election of three electors, "one in the district of Washington, one in the district of Hamilton, and one in the district of Mero," and, "that the said electors may be elected with as little trouble to the citizens as possible," certain persons of the counties of Washington, Sullivan, Green, and Hawkins were named in the act and appointed electors to elect an elector for the district of Washington; certain other persons of the counties of Knox, Jefferson, Sevier, and Blount were by name appointed to elect an elector for the district of Hamilton; and certain others of the counties of Davidson, Sumner, and Tennessee to elect an elector for the district of Mero. Laws Tenn. 1794, 1803, p. 109; Acts 2d Sess. 1st Gen. Assembly Tenn. c. 4. Electors were chosen by the persons thus designated.

In the fourth presidential election, Virginia, under the advice of Mr. Jefferson, adopted the general ticket, at least "until some uniform mode of choosing a President and Vice-President of the United States shall be prescribed by an amendment to the Constitution." Laws Va. 1799, 1800, p. 3.

Massachusetts passed a resolution providing that the electors of that State should be appointed by joint ballot of the senate and house. Mass. Resolves, June, 1800, p. 13. Pennsylvania appointed by the legislature, and upon a contest between the senate and house, the latter was forced to yield to the senate in agreeing to an arrangement which resulted in dividing the vote of the electors. 26 Niles' Reg. 17. Six States, however, chose electors by popular vote, Rhode Island supplying the place of Pennsylvania, which had theretofore followed that course. Tennessee, by act of October 26, 1799, designated persons by name to choose its three electors as under the act of 1796. Laws Tenn. 1794-1803, p. 211; Acts 2d Sess. 2d Gen. Ass. Tenn. c. 46.

Without pursuing the subject further, it is sufficient to observe that, while most of the States adopted the general ticket system, the district method obtained in Kentucky until 1824; in Tennessee and Maryland until 1832; in Indiana in 1824 and 1828; in Illinois in 1820 and 1824; and in Maine in 1820, 1824 and 1828. Massachusetts used the general ticket system in 1804, (Mass. Resolves, June, 1804, p. 19;) chose electors by joint ballot of the legislature in 1808 and in 1816, (Mass. Resolves, 1808, pp. 205, 207, 209; 1816, p. 233;) used the district system again in 1812 and in 1820, (Mass. Resolves, 1812, p. 94; 1820, p. 245;) and returned to the general ticket system in 1824, (Mass. Resolves, 1824, p. 40.) In New York the electors were elected in 1828 by districts, the district electors choosing the electors at large. N.Y. Rev. Stat. 1827, Part I, Title vi, c. 6. The appointment of electors by the legislature, instead of by popular vote, was made use of by North Carolina, Vermont and New Jersey in 1812.

In 1824 the electors were chosen by popular vote, by districts, and by general ticket, in all the States excepting Delaware, Georgia, Louisiana, New York, South Carolina, and Vermont, where they were still chosen by the legislature. After 1832 electors were chosen by general ticket in all the States excepting South Carolina, where the legislature chose them up to and including 1860. Journals 1860, Senate pp. 12, 13; House, 11, 15, 17. And this was the mode adopted by Florida in 1868, (Laws 1868, p. 166,) and by Colorado in 1876, as prescribed by § 19 of the schedule to the constitution of the State, which was admitted into the Union August 1, 1876. Gen. Laws Colorado, 1877, pp. 79, 990.

Mr. Justice Story, in considering the subject in his Commentaries on the Constitution, and writing nearly fifty years after the adoption of that instrument, after stating that "in some States the legislatures have directly chosen the electors by themselves; in others, they have been chosen by the people by a general ticket throughout the whole State; and in others, by the people by electoral districts, fixed by the legislature, a certain number of electors being apportioned to each district," adds: "No question has ever arisen as to the constitutionality of either mode, except that by a direct choice by the legislature. But this, though often doubted by able and ingenious minds, (3 Elliot's Deb. 100, 101,) has been firmly established in practice ever since the adoption of the Constitution, and does not now seem to admit of controversy, even if a suitable tribunal existed to adjudicate upon it." And he remarks that "it has been thought desirable by many statesmen to have the Constitution amended so as to provide for a uniform mode of choice by the people." Story Const. 1st Ed. § 1466.

Such an amendment was urged at the time of the adoption of the Twelfth Amendment, the suggestion being that all electors should be chosen by popular vote, the States to be divided for that purpose into districts. It was brought up again in Congress in December, 1813, but the resolution for submitting the amendment failed to be carried. The amendment was renewed in the House of Representatives in December, 1816, and a provision for the division of the States into single districts for the choice of electors received a majority vote, but not two-thirds. Like amendments were offered in the Senate by Messrs. Sanford of New York, Dickerson of New Jersey and Macon of North Carolina. December 11, 1823, Senator Benton introduced an amendment providing that each legislature should divide its State into electoral districts, and that the voters of each district "should vote, in their own proper persons," for President and Vice-President, but it was not acted upon. December 16, and December 24, 1823, amendments were introduced in the Senate by Messrs. Dickerson of New Jersey and Van Buren of New York, requiring the choice of electors to be by districts; but these and others failed of adoption, although there was favorable action in that direction by the Senate in 1818, 1819 and 1822. December 22, 1823, an amendment was introduced in the House by Mr. McDuffie of South Carolina, providing that electors should be chosen by districts assigned by the legislatures, but action was not taken. The subject was again brought forward in 1835, 1844, and subsequently, but need not be further dwelt upon, except that it may be added that, on the 28th of May, 1874, a report was made by Senator Morton, chairman of the Senate Committee on Privileges and Elections, recommending an amendment dividing the States into electoral districts, and that the majority of the popular vote of each district should give the candidate one presidential vote, but this also failed to obtain action. In this report it was said: "The appointment of these electors is thus placed absolutely and wholly with the legislatures of the several States. They may be chosen by the legislature, or the legislature may provide that they shall be elected by the people of the State at large, or in districts, as are members of Congress, which was the case formerly in many States; and it is, no doubt, competent for the legislature to authorize the governor, or the Supreme Court of the State, or any other agent of its will, to appoint these electors. This power is conferred upon the legislatures of the States by the Constitution of the United States, and cannot be taken from them or modified by their State constitutions any more than can their power to elect Senators of the United States. Whatever provisions may be made by statute, or by the state constitution, to choose electors by the people, there is no doubt of the right of the legislature to resume the power at any time, for it can neither be taken away nor abdicated." Senate Rep. 1st Sess. 43 Cong. No. 395.

From this review, in which we have been assisted by the laborious research of counsel, and which might have been greatly expanded, it is seen that from the formation of the government until now the practical construction of the clause has conceded plenary power to the state legislatures in the matter of the appointment of electors.

Even in the heated controversy of 1876-1877 the electoral vote of Colorado cast by electors chosen by the legislature passed unchallenged; and our attention has not been drawn to any previous attempt to submit to the courts the determination of the constitutionality of state action.

In short, the appointment and mode of appointment of electors belong exclusively to the States under the Constitution of the United States. They are, as remarked by Mr. Justice Gray in In re Green, 134 U.S. 377, 379, "no more officers or agents of the United States than are the members of the state legislatures when acting as electors of Federal senators, or the people of the States when acting as the electors of representatives in Congress." Congress is empowered to determine the time of choosing the electors and the day on which they are to give their votes, which is required to be the same day throughout the United States, but otherwise the power and jurisdiction of the State is exclusive, with the exception of the provisions as to the number of electors and the ineligibility of certain persons, so framed that Congressional and Federal influence might be excluded.

The question before us is not one of policy but of power, and while public opinion had gradually brought all the States as matter of fact to the pursuit of a uniform system of popular election by general ticket, that fact does not tend to weaken the force of contemporaneous and long continued previous practice when and as different views of expediency prevailed. The prescription of the written law cannot be overthrown because the States have latterly exercised in a particular way a power which they might have exercised in some other way. The construction to which we have referred has prevailed too long and been too uniform to justify us in interpreting the language of the Constitution as conveying any other meaning than that heretofore ascribed, and it must be treated as decisive.

It is argued that the district mode of choosing electors, while not obnoxious to constitutional objection, if the operation of the electoral system had conformed to its original object and purpose, had become so in view of the practical working of that system. Doubtless it was supposed that the electors would exercise a reasonable independence and fair judgment in the selection of the Chief Executive, but experience soon demonstrated that, whether chosen by the legislatures or by popular suffrage on general ticket or in districts, they were so chosen simply to register the will of the appointing power in respect of a particular candidate. In relation, then, to the independence of the electors the original expectation may be said to have been frustrated. Miller on Const. Law, 149; Rawle on Const. 55; Story Const. § 1473; The Federalist, No. 68. But we can perceive no reason for holding that the power confided to the States by the Constitution has ceased to exist because the operation of the system has not fully realized the hopes of those by whom it was created. Still less can we recognize the doctrine, that because the Constitution has been found in the march of time sufficiently comprehensive to be applicable to conditions not within the minds of its framers, and not arising in their time, it may, therefore, be wrenched from the subjects expressly embraced within it, and amended by judicial decision without action by the designated organs in the mode by which alone amendments can be made.

Nor are we able to discover any conflict between this act and the Fourteenth and Fifteenth Amendments to the Constitution.

* * *

If presidential electors are appointed by the legislatures, no discrimination is made; if they are elected in districts where each citizen has an equal right to vote the same as any other citizen has, no discrimination is made. Unless the authority vested in the legislatures by the second clause of section 1 of Article II has been divested and the State has lost its power of appointment, except in one manner, the position taken on behalf of relators is untenable, and it is apparent that neither of these amendments can be given such effect.

RAY v. BLAIR
343 U.S. 214 (1952)

[The State of Alabama permitted political parties to require candidates for the office of presidential elector to take a pledge to support the nominee of the party.]

MR. JUSTICE REED delivered the opinion of the Court.

The Supreme Court of Alabama upheld a peremptory writ of mandamus requiring the petitioner, the chairman of that state's Executive Committee of the Democratic Party, to certify respondent Edmund Blair, a member of that party, to the Secretary of State of Alabama as a candidate for Presidential Elector in the Democratic Primary to be held May 6, 1952. Respondent Blair was admittedly qualified as a candidate except that he refused to include the following quoted words in the pledge required of party candidates— a pledge to aid and support "the nominees of the National Convention of the Democratic Party for President and Vice-President of the United States." The chairman's refusal of certification was based on that omission.

* * *

As is well known, political parties in the modern sense were not born with the Republic. They were created by necessity, by the need to organize the rapidly increasing population, scattered over our Land, so as to coordinate efforts to secure needed legislation and oppose that deemed undesirable. Compare Bryce, Modern Democracies, p. 546. The party conventions of locally chosen delegates, from the county to the national level, succeeded the caucuses of self-appointed legislators or other interested individuals. Dissatisfaction with the manipulation of conventions caused that system to be largely superseded by the direct primary. This was particularly true in the South because, with the predominance of the Democratic Party in that section, the nomination was more important than the election. There primaries are generally, as in Alabama, optional. Various tests of party allegiance for candidates in direct primaries are found in a number of states. The requirement of a pledge from the candidate participating in primaries to support the nominee is not unusual. Such a provision protects a party from intrusion by those with adverse political principles. It was under the authority of § 347 of the Alabama Code, note 2, supra, that the State Democratic Executive Committee of Alabama adopted a resolution on January 26, 1952, requiring candidates in its primary to pledge support to the nominees of the National Convention of the Democratic Party for President and Vice-President. It is this provision in the qualifications required by the party under § 347 which the Supreme Court of Alabama held unconstitutional in this case.

The opinion of the Supreme Court of Alabama concluded that the Executive Committee requirement violated the Twelfth Amendment, note 1, supra. It said:

"We appreciate the argument that from time immemorial, the electors selected to vote in the college have voted in accordance with the wishes of the party to which they belong. But in doing so, the effective compulsion has been party loyalty. That theory has generally been taken for granted, so that the voting for a president and vice-president has been usually formal merely. But the Twelfth Amendment does not make it so. The nominees of the party for president and vice-president may have become disqualified, or peculiarly offensive not only to the electors but their constituents also. They should be free to vote for another, as contemplated by the Twelfth Amendment." 257 Ala., at , 57 So. 2d, at 398.

In urging a contrary view the dissenting Alabama justices, in supporting the right of the Committee to require this candidate to pledge support to the party nominees, said:

"Any other view, it seems, would destroy effective party government and would privilege any candidate, regardless of his political persuasion, to enter a primary election as a candidate for elector and fix his own qualifications for such candidacy. This is contrary to the traditional American political system." 257 Ala., at , 57 So. 2d, at 403.

The applicable constitutional provisions on their face furnish no definite answer to the query whether a state may permit a party to require party regularity from its primary candidates for national electors. The presidential electors exercise a federal function in balloting for President and Vice-President but they are not federal officers or agents any more than the state elector who votes for congressmen. They act by authority of the state that in turn receives its authority from the Federal Constitution.

Neither the language of Art. II, § 1, nor that of the Twelfth Amendment forbids a party to require from candidates in its primary a pledge of political conformity with the aims of the party. Unless such a requirement is implicit, certainly neither provision of the Constitution requires a state political party, affiliated with a national party through acceptance of the national call to send state delegates to the national convention, to accept persons as candidates who refuse to agree to abide by the party's requirement.

The argument against the party's power to exclude as candidates in the primary those unwilling to agree to aid and support the national nominees runs as follows: The constitutional method for the selection of the President and Vice-President is for states to appoint electors who shall in turn vote for our chief executives. The intention of the Founders was that those electors should exercise their judgment in voting for President and Vice-President. Therefore this requirement of a pledge is a restriction in substance, if not in form, that interferes with the performance of this constitutional duty to select the proper persons to head the Nation, according to the best judgment of the elector.

* * *

[W]e [next] consider the argument that the Twelfth Amendment demands absolute freedom for the elector to vote his own choice, uninhibited by a pledge. It is true that the Amendment says the electors shall vote by ballot. But it is also true that the Amendment does not prohibit an elector's announcing his choice beforehand, pledging himself. The suggestion that in the early elections candidates for electors—contemporaries of the Founders—would have hesitated, because of constitutional limitations, to pledge themselves to support party nominees in the event of their selection as electors is impossible to accept. History teaches that the electors were expected to support the party nominees. Experts in the history of government recognize the longstanding practice. Indeed, more than twenty states do not print the names of the candidates for electors on the general election ballot. Instead, in one form or another, they allow a vote for the presidential candidate of the national conventions to be counted as a vote for his party's nominees for the electoral college. This long-continued practical interpretation of the constitutional propriety of an implied or oral pledge of his ballot by a candidate for elector as to his vote in the electoral college weighs heavily in considering the constitutionality of a pledge, such as the one here required, in the primary.

However, even if such promises of candidates for the electoral college are legally unenforceable because violative of an assumed constitutional freedom of the elector under the Constitution, Art. II, § 1, to vote as he may choose in the electoral college, it would not follow that the requirement of a pledge in the primary is unconstitutional. A candidacy in the primary is a voluntary act of the applicant. He is not barred, discriminatorily, from participating but must comply with the rules of the party. Surely one may voluntarily assume obligations to vote for a certain candidate. The state offers him opportunity to become a candidate for elector on his own terms, although he must file his declaration before the primary. Ala. Code, Tit. 17, § 145. Even though the victory of an independent candidate for elector in Alabama cannot be anticipated, the state does offer the opportunity for the development of other strong political organizations where the need is felt for them by a sizable block of voters. Such parties may leave their electors to their own choice.

We conclude that the Twelfth Amendment does not bar a political party from requiring the pledge to support the nominees of the National Convention. Where a state authorizes a party to choose its nominees for elector in a party primary and to fix the qualifications for the candidates, we see no federal constitutional objection to the requirement of this pledge.

MR. JUSTICE BLACK took no part in the consideration or decision of this case.

MR. JUSTICE FRANKFURTER, not having heard the argument, owing to illness, took no part in the disposition of the case.

MR. JUSTICE JACKSON, with whom MR. JUSTICE DOUGLAS joins, dissenting.

The Constitution and its Twelfth Amendment allow each State, in its own way, to name electors with such personal qualifications, apart from stated disqualifications, as the State prescribes. Their number, the time that they shall be named, the manner in which the State must certify their ascertainment and the determination of any contest are prescribed by federal law. U.S. Const., Art. II, § 1, 3 U. S. C. §§ 1-7. When chosen, they perform a federal function of balloting for President and Vice President, federal law prescribing the time of meeting, the manner of certifying "all the votes given by them," and in detail how such certificates shall be transmitted and counted. U.S. Const., Amend. XII, 3 U. S. C. §§ 9-20. But federal statute undertakes no control of their votes beyond providing "The electors shall vote for President and Vice President, respectively, in the manner directed by the Constitution," 3 U. S. C. § 8, and the Constitution requires only that they "vote by ballot for President and Vice-President, one of whom, at least, shall not be an inhabitant of the same state with themselves." U.S. Const., Amend. XII. No one faithful to our history can deny that the plan originally contemplated, what is implicit in its text, that electors would be free agents, to exercise an independent and nonpartisan judgment as to the men best qualified for the Nation's highest offices. Certainly under that plan no state law could control the elector in performance of his federal duty, any more than it could a United States Senator who also is chosen by, and represents, the State.

This arrangement miscarried. Electors, although often personally eminent, independent, and respectable, officially became voluntary party lackeys and intellectual nonentities to whose memory we might justly paraphrase a tuneful satire:

> They always voted at their Party's call
> And never thought of thinking for themselves at all.
> As an institution the Electoral College suffered
> atrophy almost indistinguishable from rigor mortis.

However, in 1948, Alabama's Democratic Party Electors refused to vote for the nominee of the Democratic National Convention. To put an end to such party unreliability the party organization, exercising state-delegated authority, closed the official primary to any candidate for elector unless he would pledge himself, under oath, to support any candidate named by the Democratic National Convention. It is conceded that under long-prevailing conditions this effectively forecloses any chance of the State being represented by an unpledged elector. In effect, before one can become an elector for Alabama, its law requires that he must pawn his ballot to a candidate not yet named, by a convention not yet held, of delegates not yet chosen. Even if the nominee repudiates the platform adopted by the same convention, as Democratic nominees have twice done in my lifetime (1904, 1928), the elector is bound to vote for him. It will be seen that the State has sought to achieve control of the electors' ballots. But the balloting cannot be constitutionally subjected to any such control because it was intended to be free, an act performed after all functions of the electoral process left to the States have been completed. The Alabama Supreme Court held that such a requirement violates the Federal Constitution, and I agree.

It may be admitted that this law does no more than to make a legal obligation of what has been a voluntary general practice. If custom were sufficient authority for amendment of the Constitution by Court decree, the decision in this matter would be warranted. Usage may sometimes impart changed content to constitutional generalities, such as "due process of law," "equal protection," or "commerce among the states." But I do not think powers or discretions granted to federal officials by the Federal Constitution can be forfeited by the Court for disuse. A political practice which has its origin in custom must rely upon custom for its sanctions.

The demise of the whole electoral system would not impress me as a disaster. At its best it is a mystifying and distorting factor in presidential elections which may resolve a popular defeat into an electoral victory. At its worst it is open to local corruption and manipulation, once so flagrant as to threaten the stability of the country. To abolish it and substitute direct election of the President, so that every vote wherever cast would have equal weight in calculating the result, would seem to me a gain for simplicity and integrity of our governmental processes.

But the Court's decision does not even move in that direction. What it is doing is to entrench the worst features of the system in constitutional law and to elevate the perversion of the forefathers' plan into a constitutional principle. This judicial overturn of the theory that has come down to us cannot plead the excuse that it is a practical remedy for the evils or weaknesses of the system.

The Court is sanctioning a new instrument of power in the hands of any faction that can get control of the Democratic National Convention to make it sure of Alabama's electoral vote. When the party is in power this will likely be the administration faction and when not in power no one knows what group it will be. This device of prepledged and oath-bound electors imposes upon the party within the State an oath-bound regularity and loyalty to the controlling element in the national party. It centralizes party control and, instead of securing for the locality a share in the central management, it secures the central management in dominance of the local vote in the Electoral College. If we desire free elections, we should not add to the leverage over local party representatives always possessed by those who enjoy the prestige and dispense the patronage of a national administration.

The view of many that it is the progressive or liberal element of the party that will presently advantage from this device does not prove that the device itself has any proper place in a truly liberal or progressive scheme of government. Who will come to possess this weapon and to whose advantage it will prove in the long run I am not foresighted enough to predict. But party control entrenched by disfranchisement and exclusion of nonconforming party members is a means which to my mind cannot be justified by any end. In the interest of free government, we should foster the power and the will to be independent even on the part of those we may think to be independently wrong.

Candidates for elector, like those for Senator, of course, may announce to their constituents their policies and preferences, and assume a moral duty to carry them out if they are chosen. Competition in the primary between those of different views would forward the representative principle. But this plan effects a complete suppression of competition between different views within the party. All who are not ready to follow blindly anyone chosen by the national convention are excluded from the primary, and that, in practice, means also from the election.

It is not for me, as a judge, to pass upon the wisdom or righteousness of the political revolt this measure was designed to suppress. For me it is enough that, be it ever so benevolent and virtuous, the end cannot justify these means.

I would affirm the decision of the Supreme Court of Alabama.

Rules of the U.S.
House of Representatives

[Rules adopted in 1801 to govern the election of a president of the United States by the House of Representatives.]

1. In the event of its appearing, upon the counting and ascertaining of the votes given for President and Vice-President, according to the mode prescribed by the Constitution, that no person has a constitutional majority, and the same shall have been duly declared and entered on the journals of this House, the Speaker, accompanied by the Members of the House, shall return to their Chamber.

2. Seats shall be provided in this House for the President and members of the Senate and notification of the same shall be made to the Senate.

3. The House, on their return from the Senate Chamber, it being ascertained that the constitutional number of States are present, shall immediately proceed to choose one of the persons from whom the choice is to be made for President; and in case upon the first ballot there shall not appear to be a majority of the States in favor of one of them, in such case the House shall continue to ballot for a President, without interruption by other business, until it shall appear that a President is duly chosen.

4. After commencing the balloting for President, the House shall not adjourn until a choice be made.

5. The doors of the House shall be closed during the balloting, except against the officers of the House.

6. In balloting, the following mode shall be observed, to wit: The Representatives of the respective States shall be so seated that the delegation of each State shall be together. The Representatives of each State shall, in the first instance, ballot among themselves, in order to ascertain the votes of the State, and it shall be allowed,

where deemed necessary by the delegation, to name one or more persons of the representation to be tellers of the ballots. After the vote of each State is ascertained, duplicates thereof shall be made; and in case the vote of the State be for one person, then the name of that person shall be written on each of the duplicates; and in case the ballots of the State be equally divided, then the word "divided" shall be written on each duplicate, and the said duplicates shall be deposited in manner hereafter prescribed, in boxes to be provided. That, for the conveniently taking the ballots of the several Representatives of the respective States, there be sixteen ballot boxes provided; and that there be additionally two boxes provided for the purpose of receiving the votes of the States; that after the delegation of each State shall have ascertained the vote of the State, the Sergeant-at-Arms shall carry to the respective delegations the two ballot boxes, and the delegation of each State, in the presence and subject to the examination of all the members of the delegation, shall deposit a duplicate of the vote of the State in each ballot box; and where there is more than one Representative of a State the duplicates shall not both be deposited by the same person. When the votes of the States are all thus taken in, the Sergeant-at-Arms shall carry one of the general ballot boxes to one table and the other to a second and separate table. Sixteen members shall then be appointed as tellers of the ballots, one of whom shall be taken from each State, and be nominated by the delegation of the State from which he was taken. The said tellers shall be divided into two equal sets, according to such agreement as shall be made among themselves, and one of the said sets of tellers shall proceed to count the votes in one of the said boxes and the other set the votes in the other box; and in the event of no appointment of teller by any delegation, the Speaker shall in such case appoint. When the votes of the States are counted by the respective sets of tellers, the result shall be reported to the House; and if the reports agree, the same shall be accepted as the true votes of the States; but if the reports disagree, the States shall immediately proceed to a new ballot in manner aforesaid.

7. If either of the persons voted for shall have a majority of the votes of all the States the Speaker shall declare the same, and official notice thereof shall be immediately given to the President of the United States and to the Senate.

8. All questions which shall arise after the balloting commences, and which shall be decided by the House voting per capita, to be

incidental to the power of choosing the President, and which shall require the decision of the House, shall be decided by States, and without debate; and in case of an equal division of the votes of States, the question shall be lost.

[Rules adopted in 1825 to govern the voting for a president of the United States when the election was thrown into the House by the failure of the electoral college to make a choice that year.]

1. In the event of its appearing, on opening all the certificates, and counting the votes given by the electors of the several States for President, that no person has a majority of the votes of the whole number of electors appointed, the same shall be entered on the Journals of this House.

2. The roll of the House shall then be called by States; and, on its appearing that a Member or Members from two-thirds of the States are present, the House shall immediately proceed, by ballot, to choose a President from the persons having the highest numbers, not exceeding three, on the list of those voted for as President; and, in case neither of those persons shall receive the votes of a majority of all the States on the first ballot, the House shall continue to ballot for a President, without interruption by other business, until a President be chosen.

3. The doors of the Hall shall be closed during the balloting, except against the Members of the Senate, stenographers, and the officers of the House.

4. From the commencement of the balloting until an election is made no proposition to adjourn shall be received, unless on the motion of one State, seconded by another State, and the question shall be decided by States. The same rule shall be observed in regard to any motion to change the usual hour for the meeting of the House.

5. In balloting the following mode shall be observed, to wit:

The Representatives of each State shall be arranged and seated together, beginning with the seats at the right hand of the Speaker's chair, with the Members from the State of Maine; thence, proceeding with the Members from the States, in the order the States are usually named for receiving petitions, around the Hall of the House, until all are seated.

A ballot box shall be provided for each State.

The Representatives of each State shall, in the first instance, ballot among themselves, in order to ascertain the vote of their State; and they may, if necessary, appoint tellers of their ballots.

After the vote of each State is ascertained, duplicates thereof shall be made out; and in case any one of the persons from whom the choice is to be made shall receive a majority of the votes given, on any one balloting by the Representatives of a State, the name of that person shall be written on each of the duplicates; and in case the votes so given shall be divided so that neither of said persons shall have a majority of the whole number of votes given by such State, on any one balloting, then the word "divided" shall be written on each duplicate.

After the delegation from each State shall have ascertained the vote of their State, the Clerk shall name the States in the order they are usually named for receiving petitions; and as the name of each is called the Sergeant-at-Arms shall present to the delegation of each two ballot boxes, in each of which shall be deposited, by some Representative of the State, one of the duplicates made as aforesaid of the vote of said State, in the presence and subject to the examination of all the Members from said State then present; and where there is more than one Representative from a State, the duplicates shall not both be deposited by the same person.

When the votes of the States are thus all taken in, the Sergeant-at-Arms shall carry one of said ballot boxes to one table and the other to a separate and distinct table.

One person from each State represented in the balloting shall be appointed by the Representatives to tell off said ballots; but, in case the Representatives fail to appoint a teller, the Speaker shall appoint.

The said tellers shall divide themselves into two sets, as nearly equal in number as can be, and one of the said sets of tellers shall proceed to count the votes in one of said boxes, and the other set the votes in the other box.

When the votes are counted by the different sets of tellers, the result shall be reported to the House; and if the reports agree, the same shall be accepted as the true votes of the States; but if the reports disagree, the States shall proceed, in the same manner as before, to a new ballot.

6. All questions arising after the balloting commences, requiring the decision of the House, which shall be decided by the House,

voting per capita, to be incidental to the power of choosing a President, shall be decided by States without debate; and in case of an equal division of the votes of States, the question shall be lost.

7. When either of the persons from whom the choice is to be made shall have received a majority of all the States, the Speaker shall declare the same, and that that person is elected President of the United States.

8. The result shall be immediately communicated to the Senate by message, and a committee of three persons shall be appointed to inform the President of the United States and the President-elect of said election.

Select Bibliography

Select Bibliography

American Bar Association. *Electing the President: A Report of the Commission on Electoral Reform*. Chicago: American Bar Association, 1967.

Association of the Bar of the City of New York. *Report of the Committee on Federal Legislation: Proposed Constitutional Amendment Abolishing the Electoral College and Making Other Changes in the Election of the President and Vice-President*. New York: Association of the Bar of the City of New York, 1969.

Banzhaf, John F., III. "One Man, 3.312 Votes: A Mathematical Analysis of the Electoral College." *Villanova Law Review* 13 (Winter 1968): 304-322.

Bayh, Birch. "Electing a President: The Case for Direct Popular Election." *Harvard Journal on Legislation* (January 1969): 1-12.

Beman, L. T. *Abolishment of the Electoral College*. New York: H. W. Wilson, 1926.

Best, Judith. *The Case against Direct Election of the President: A Defense of the Electoral College*. Ithaca, N.Y.: Cornell University Press, 1975.

Bickel, Alexander M. *Reform and Continuity: The Electoral College, the Convention and the Party System*. New York: Harper and Row, 1968.

Congressional Quarterly Inc. *Congressional Quarterly's Guide to Congress*. 4th ed. Washington, D.C.: Congressional Quarterly Inc., 1991.

Congressional Quarterly Inc. *Congressional Quarterly's Guide to Elections*. 2d ed. Washington, D.C.: Congressional Quarterly Inc., 1985.

Congressional Research Service. American Law Division. "Majority of Plurality Vote within State Delegations When House of Representatives Votes for the President." Congressional Research Service, Washington, D.C., June 10, 1980.

Diamond, Martin. *The Electoral College and the American Idea of Democracy.* Washington, D.C.: American Enterprise Institute, 1977.

Durbin, Thomas M. "The Electoral College Method of Electing the President and Vice President and Proposals for Reform." Congressional Research Service, Washington, D.C., August 8, 1988.

――――. "The 1992 Electoral College Dilemma: The H. Ross Perot Factor." Congressional Research Service, American Law Division, Washington, D.C., undated.

Durbin, Thomas M., and L. Paige Whitaker. "Nomination and Election of the President and Vice President of the United States, 1992." Congressional Research Service, Washington, D.C., January 1992.

Feerick, John D. "The Electoral College: Why It Ought to Be Abolished." *Fordham Law Review* (October 1968): 43.

Freund, Paul A. "Direct Election of the President: Issues and Answers." *American Bar Association Journal* (August 1970): 733.

Frost, Martin. "Election of the President in the House of Representatives." Unpublished memorandum to Richard Bolling, July 1, 1980.

Galvin, Thomas. "House Warily Dusts Off Rules on Choosing a President." *Congressional Quarterly Weekly Report,* May 23, 1992, 1420.

Gorman, Joseph. "Election of the President by the House of Representatives and the Vice President by the Senate: Relationship of the Popular Vote for Electors to Subsequent Voting in the House of Representatives in 1801 and 1825 and in the Senate in 1837." Congressional Research Service, Washington, D.C., November 20, 1980.

Government and General Research Division. "Election of the President by the House of Representatives." Congressional Research Service, Washington, D.C., August 19, 1968; rev. February 6, 1969.

Hinds, Asher C. *Hinds' Precedents of the House of Representatives of the United States.* Washington, D.C.: Government Printing Office, 1907.

Huckabee, David C. "Electoral Votes Based on the 1990 Census."

Congressional Research Service, Washington, D.C., November 19, 1991.

League of Women Voters. *Who Should Elect the President?* Washington, D.C.: League of Women Voters of the United States, 1969.

Longley, Lawrence D. "The Electoral College." *Current History* 67 (August 1974): 64.

Longley, Lawrence D., and Alan G. Braun. *The Politics of Electoral College Reform.* 2d ed. New Haven, Conn.: Yale University Press, 1975.

Michener, James A. *Presidential Lottery: The Reckless Gamble in Our Electoral System.* New York: Random House, 1969.

Neale, Thomas H. "Contingent Election: Congress Elects the President and Vice President." Congressional Research Service, Washington, D.C., May 20, 1992.

———. "Presidential Elections in the United States." Congressional Research Service, Washington, D.C., June 6, 1991.

Nelson, Michael, ed. *Guide to the Presidency.* Washington, D.C.: Congressional Quarterly Inc., 1989.

Nicola, Thomas J. "Meaning and Implications of Twelfth Amendment Requirement that House Vote for President 'by Ballot.'" Congressional Research Service, Washington, D.C., June 10, 1980.

Peirce, Neal R., and Lawrence D. Longley. *The People's President: The Electoral College in American History and the Direct-Vote Alternative.* Rev. ed. New Haven, Conn.: Yale University Press, 1981.

Polsby, Nelson, and Aaron Wildavsky. *Presidential Elections.* 4th ed. New York: Scribner's, 1976.

Relyea, Harold C. "Federal Presidential Libraries." Congressional Research Service, Washington, D.C., December 14, 1990.

Sayre, Wallace S., and Judith H. Parris. *Voting for President: The Electoral College and the American Political System.* Washington, D.C.: Brookings, 1970.

Schlesinger, Arthur M., Jr., ed. *The Coming to Power: Critical Presidential Elections in American History.* New York: McGraw-Hill, 1972.

Sievers, H. J. "Reform of the Electoral College." *America,* November 16, 1968, 465.

Silva, Ruth C. "Reform of the Electoral College." *Review of Politics* (July 1952): 397.

Tipy, Thomas B. "Would the District of Columbia Be Allowed to Vote in the Selection of a President by the House of Representatives?" Congressional Research Service, Washington, D.C., July 7, 1980.

Tribe, Laurence H., and Thomas M. Rollins. "Deadlock: What Happens If Nobody Wins." *Atlantic Monthly,* October 1980, 49.

Twentieth Century Fund. *Winner Take All: Report of the Twentieth Century Fund Task Force on Reform of the Presidential Election Process.* New York: Holmes & Meier, 1978.

U.S. Senate. Committee on the Judiciary. *Hearings on the Electoral College and Direct Election.* 95th Cong., 1st sess. Washington, D.C.: Government Printing Office, 1977.

U.S. Senate. Committee on the Judiciary. Subcommittee on the Constitution. *Direct Popular Election of the President and Vice President of the United States.* Hearings, 96th Cong., 1st sess., on S.J. Res. 28, March 27-April 9, 1979. Washington, D.C.: Government Printing Office, 1979.

Walser, George. "Electoral College: Bibliography-in-Brief, 1958-1988." Congressional Research Service, Washington, D.C., October 1988.

Weinhagen, Robert F., Jr. "Should the Electoral College Be Abandoned?" *American Bar Association Journal* 67 (July 1981): 852-857.

Wilmerding, Lucius, Jr. *The Electoral College.* New Brunswick, N.J.: Rutgers University Press, 1958.

Wroth, L. Kinvin. "Election Contests and the Electoral Vote." *Dickinson Law Review* 65 (1960-61): 321-353.

Yunker, John H., and Lawrence D. Longley. "The Biases of the Electoral College: Who Is Really Advantaged?" In *Perspectives on Presidential Selection,* ed. Donald R. Matthews. Washington, D.C.: Brookings, 1973.

Index

Index